Coggeshall's Voyages

Coggeshall's Voyages
The Recollections of an
American Schooner Captain

George Coggeshall

LEONAUR

Coggeshall's Voyages
The Recollections of an American
Schooner Captain
by George Coggeshall

First published under the title
Voyages

Leonaur is an imprint
of Oakpast Ltd

ISBN: 978-1-84677-672-4 (hardcover)
ISBN: 978-1-84677-671-7 (softcover)

http://www.leonaur.com

Publisher's Notes

In the interests of authenticity, the spellings, grammar and place names
used have been retained from the original editions.

The opinions of the authors represent a view of events in which he
was a participant related from his own perspective,
as such the text is relevant as an historical document.

The views expressed in this book are not necessarily
those of the publisher.

Contents

GEORGE COGGESHALL

To Benjamin Silliman, LL. D.,
Professor of Chemistry and Geology, Yale College.
My Dear Sir:

One of the most cherished attainments of my life is your friendship. Nothing could be less similar than our pursuits; but I am proud to know that, notwithstanding the rough and stormy life that I have led, you have been pleased to recognize in me enough to secure your regard and confidence. As a slight token of how sincerely I reciprocate the kind feelings you have ever manifested for me, I beg leave to inscribe to you the following pages.

Since I have retired from the sea and become an old man, it has been a gratification to me, occasionally to re-peruse my journals, and though I have had few "battles" to "fight o'er again," yet I have had some conflicts with the elements, and many with fortune—the narration of which, my friends advise me, may be not altogether uninteresting to the public. I need not say that the style of my book is unadorned. It consists of the simple record, in plain seaman's phrase, of occurrences, which, when written, I thought might interest my family, but which were preserved with reference to no other readers.

Maturer years and more leisure have shown me that they are quite devoid of literary merit, but I have not thought it best to rewrite them, lest by attempting to beautify I should enfeeble my work. If it fails to entertain, I trust it will at least have no evil influence on others; and should it receive your approbation, nothing connected with it will be more welcome to

Your very sincere friend and obedient servant,
George Coggeshall.
New York, March, 1851.

Preface

It may disarm criticism of some of its asperity, when the author states that, in publishing for the entertainment of his friends the following extracts from his journal, he makes no pretensions to literary skill or merit. His life has been passed in ploughing the ocean, and not in cultivating the delightful and peaceful fields of learning.

In selecting for publication the *Voyages* (written at the periods to which they relate) contained in this volume, he has aimed at presenting a fair specimen of the toils and perils in which his many years have been passed. They may interest others, and perhaps serve to show to the young and inexperienced, that by keeping a stout heart and persevering spirit, that degree of success may be counted on which will secure personal independence, and the ability to do something for the happiness of others.

In these quiet days of peace, when war, with its excitements, and violence, and sorrows, is unknown among us, some of its legitimate and necessary features are viewed with a degree of disfavour, quite unfelt at the time of its existence. This is especially true as regards privateers and letters-of-marque. All wars have for their immediate object the annoyance of the enemy. Between maritime states, the destruction of each other's commerce is the aim of the belligerents. In our last war with Great Britain (to which several chapters in this volume relate), the most active agents in crippling the commerce of the enemy, were those of the private armed service. The efficiency and daring gallantry of our privateers were eminently conspicuous. True it is that much danger exists of abuses in this branch of service, and that cruelty to prisoners, and mere cupidity, occasionally marked its course during the war. But it should be borne in mind that hardly any institution is free from liability to abuse, and that it is unjust and unphilosophical to stigmatize classes because of the faults of individuals. To do so is the common error of the ignorant and the vulgar. They do not discriminate between lawyers and pettifoggers, physicians and quacks, clergymen and hypocrites, merchants and sharpers.

No greater injustice can be done than to denounce as mere mercenaries all the young men who during our war with England embarked in the private armed service. Hundreds of my brother mariners well know that the most generous and patriotic impulses inspired hosts of brave spirits to embark in the work of combating and destroying the ships and commerce of our great rival, until we should obtain the freedom of the seas; and none who are informed on the subject are ignorant that the object was accomplished.

But it is not my intent now to vindicate the system of privateering—my book relates to another period of the world's history than the present, and though the sentiment of this day is adverse to that system, yet its excellence or immorality is not to be decided here.

To denounce the past by the lights of the present, is "to read history backwards." The acts of a former period are to be judged by the condition of the world, and of its knowledge and sentiments at that time.

Whatever difference of opinion existed as to the merits of the war with England, there can, at this day, be none as to its results. Nearly thirty-seven years have passed since the treaty of Ghent brought us peace, and the unexampled prosperity which has followed, and the pre-eminent position, both in power and in honour, which our country has attained, are due in no small degree to the gallantry and national resource manifested by us during the three years' contest.

Compare and contrast our present condition with what it was before that war. After the peace of 1783, our ships and commerce were preyed upon by England and France with impunity, and we manifested in our then feeble condition the most patient forbearance, and even submission. At length we were driven to arm against our ancient ally, France, until we compelled a recognition of our rights by the treaty of Paris in 1800.

Previous to this period our vessels trading to British ports were seized by French cruisers, carried into their own ports and condemned; and as the war between France and Britain became more embittered, both determined that there should be no longer any neutral powers if they could prevent it. They imposed restriction upon restriction on the commerce of other countries, and did everything to compel all the nations to take part in their contest. Our vessels were assailed by French decrees and British orders in council. The accustomed channels were closed. With cargoes destined for Hamburgh, I was compelled to make several voyages to Tonningen, in Danish Holstein, and when this trade was no longer permitted by France, I was forced up among the snow and ice of Russia. Such were the injuries to which we were subjected by France.

England was still more aggressive. Her cruisers captured more than one thousand ships and other vessels bound to France and other countries, which were overrun by French armies, before the United States could be driven to the declaration of war of 1812. England and France had seemed to regard our commerce as their legitimate prey, and they felt satisfied that our love of thrift and our passion for gain were paramount to our sense of honour, patriotism, and national pride.

England assumed and boasted that a few broadsides from her "wooden walls" would drive our paltry striped bunting from the ocean. Our seamen were impressed by them—our vessels searched in the most arrogant and offensive manner, and their people ill-treated. One outrage of this kind succeeded another, until one of their men-of-war fired her cowardly cannon into a harmless little unarmed vessel (April 26th, 1806,) off Sandy Hook, and one of our citizens was killed. This was followed by the crowning wrong and insult of the attack by the British frigate *Leopard* upon the American frigate *Chesapeake,* in a period of profound peace, and at a moment when from peculiar causes the latter ship was in a defenceless position.

This act roused a spirit which nothing could quell. Congress declared war in 1812 against the mightiest of the nations. But "thrice were we armed," for we "had our quarrel just." In less than three years, two entire fleets of British men-of-war were swept from the Lakes. More than fifteen hundred sail of British ships and other vessels were captured. One of our frigates vanquished two frigates of the enemy, one after the other in fair combat, and afterwards encountered at once two of their sloops-of-war with a like result. Other and gallant actions and victories followed. The spell was broken. British invincibility and British supremacy were at an end. The stars and stripes were no longer a theme of ridicule—our commerce was no longer at the mercy and conducted by the permission and sufferance of England.

Far be it from the writer of these pages to indulge in either a revengeful or a boasting spirit; but it may be permitted to one who in early life encountered so much of annoyance and injury—so much that was galling to the spirit of every man who felt that the ocean was by right the free thoroughfare of all nations—to rejoice that wherever our flag now floats it carries security, respect and honour to all beneath its folds. That the "right of search," claimed so long and exercised so arrogantly, is now abandoned—that our nation and our people know no superiors—and that we present at this moment the most remarkable spectacle the world has ever known of a free, prosperous, powerful, and educated people. Let it be our aim to bear our prosperity with moderation, with dignity, and with gratitude to the great Ruler of nations; and to remember that we shall become, base whenever we wield our power against the weak and humble, or in any cause that has not honour, truth, and justice for its foundation and its end.

CHAPTER 1

Voyage in the Schooner *Charlotte*

I was now a boy, of sixteen years of age, and had made one voyage to Cadiz in the schooner *Charlotte*. On the return of this vessel to New York, her captain and crew were all discharged, and I alone remained on board as ship-keeper at Brooklyn about two months, after which time she was removed to New York, where we commenced taking in a general cargo on freight for Savannah, under the command of Captain Crocker.

Thus I found myself among entire strangers at the commencement of a new voyage. The mate's name was Coleman. He was a young man, a native of Nantucket, who had been brought up in the whaling business, and had always been accustomed to long voyages to distant seas. He had never made one in a merchant trading vessel, and although a kind-hearted, good fellow, seemed to have very little in common with his fellowmen. Whenever a porpoise or a whale came in sight, he was in his element, and so delighted and excited that he could scarcely restrain himself, and in ecstasies cried out "townor."

Our captain had for many years commanded a packet brig between New York and Savannah, and was a very amiable man, though somewhat advanced in years. The crew consisted of six seamen, a black cook, and myself as cabin boy. We sailed from New York about the 1st of June, and had a pleasant passage of thirteen days to Savannah, without any remarkable occurrence. We soon discharged our cargo, and took on board another of tobacco and staves.

Being loaded and nearly ready for sea one morning at day-light the mate went forward to the forecastle to call all hands, when behold not a man was to be found. On searching about, we found the crew had stolen the boat, and, taking what things they could stow away in bags, were off for Charleston, which was the last we ever heard of them.

Seamen being scarce and wages high, we were obliged to take such as we could get. Among them was a "Cracker" a tall, lean-looking man, recently from the interior, and who had never before seen the salt water. Having shipped our motley crew of all colours and all nations, we sailed from Savannah on the 28th of June, 1800, for Gibraltar.

About a week or ten days after sailing, one morning at day-light, while steering to the eastward with a strong gale from the northward, we discovered a sail astern, in full chase, and, as we supposed her a French privateer, we crowded all sail to make our escape. The gale increased, we took in our fore-topsail, reefed our lower sails, and hauled close to the wind to the N. E. The chase fore-reached us, but did not hold so good a wind as our sharp schooner, so that his shot could not reach us, and he was com-pelled to tack and get again into our wake, while we crowded all the sail the schooner could bear, and kept steadily on our course, dashing through the spray like, a porpoise. At sunset she was near enough to reach us with her guns, when we set our colours and hove to. My readers may imagine our mutual disappointment when we found we both wore the Stars and Stripes. She proved to be the U. S. brig *Pickering,* of fourteen guns, Captain Preble. She had taken us for a French privateer; and the lieutenant who boarded us, said that nearly every person on board had been wet to the skin during the whole chase. After wishing them a suc-cessful cruise, we separated with mutual good wishes.

During our stay at Savannah our captain and mate were sick with the fever and ague, and it sometimes happened on our passage to Gibraltar, that neither of them were able to come on deck to take an observation of the sun. At these times, though a boy of sixteen years, I officiated to take the sun's altitude, and with a little help from the captain or mate was enabled to find the latitude. On our passage out the poor good-natured fellow from the interior of Georgia, fell sick, and was soon very much reduced in flesh, with a bad fever-sore on his right leg, which rendered him unfit for duty. I do not recollect any incident worth noting, until we arrived at Gibraltar on the 27th of July, after a passage of twenty-nine days. Our cargo was soon sold and discharged, and the vessel ballasted with sand. While lying in this port, we were often annoyed and harassed by press-gangs, headed by British naval officers, scrutinizing our protections, and often threatening and ill-treating the men. These cruelties may be overlooked and forgiven, but will ever be remembered by Americans, and for fear I should say too much, I will drop the subject.

While we were lying in this port, one morning at daylight we heard firing at a distance. I took a spy-glass, and from aloft could clearly see three gun-boats engaged with a large ship. It was a fine clear morning, with scarcely wind enough to ruffle the glass-like surface of the water. During the first hour or two of this engagement, the gun-boats had an immense advantage; being propelled both by sails and oars, they were enabled to choose their own position. While the ship lay becalmed and un-manageable, they poured grape and canister shot into her stern and bows like hailstones. At this time the ship's crew could not bring a single gun to bear upon them, and all they could do was to use their small arms through the ports and over the rails. Fortunately for the crew, the ship had thick and high bulwarks, which protected them from the fire of the enemy, so that while they were hid and screened by the boarding cloths, they could use their small arms to great advantage. At this stage of the ac-tion, while the captain with his speaking trumpet under his left arm was endeavouring to bring one of his big guns to bear on one of the gun-boats, a grapeshot passed through the port and trumpet and entered his chest near his shoulder-blade. The chief mate carried him below and laid him upon a mattress on the cabin floor. For a moment it seemed to dampen the ardour of the men; but it was but for an instant. The chief mate (I think his name was Randall), a gallant young man from Nantucket, then took the command, rallied and encouraged the men to continue the action with renewed obstinacy and vigour. At this time a lateen rigged vessel, the largest of the three privateers, was preparing to make a desperate attempt to board the ship on the larboard quarter, and, with nearly all his men on the forecastle and long bowsprit, were ready to take the final leap.

In order to meet and frustrate the design of the enemy, the mate of the ship had one of the quarter-deck guns loaded with grape and canister shot; he then ordered all the ports on this quarter to be shut, so that the gun could not be seen, and thus were both parties prepared, when the privateer came boldly up within a few yards of the ship's lee-quarter. The captain, with a threatening flourish of his sword, cried out with a loud voice in broken English, "Strike, you dammer rascal, or I will put you all to death." At this moment a diminutive looking man, on board the *Louisa,* with a musket, took deliberate aim through one of the waist ports, and shot him dead. Instantly the gun was run out and discharged upon the foe with deadly effect, so that the remaining few on board the privateer, amazed and astounded, were glad to give up the conflict, and get off the best way they could.

Soon after this, a breeze sprung up, so that they could work their great guns to some purpose. I never shall forget the moment when I saw the star-spangled banner blow out and wave gracefully in the wind, through the smoke. I also at the same moment saw with pleasure the three gun-boats sailing and rowing away towards the land to make their escape. When the ship drew near the port, all the boats from the American shipping voluntarily went to assist in bringing her to anchor, She proved to be the letter-of-marque ship *Louisa,* of Philadelphia.

I went with our captain on board of her, and we there learned that, with the exception of the captain, not a man had been killed or wounded. The ship was terribly cut up and crippled in her sails and rigging—lifts and braces shot away: her stern was literally riddled like a grater, and both large and small shot, in great numbers, had entered her hull and were sticking to her sides. How the officers and crew escaped unhurt is almost impossible to conceive. The poor captain was immediately taken on shore, but only survived his wound a few days. He had a public funeral, and was followed to the grave by all the Americans in Gibraltar, and very many of the officers of the garrison, and inhabitants of the town.

The ship had a rich cargo of coffee, sugar, and India goods, on board, and I believe was bound to Leghorn. The gun boats belonged to Algeciras, and fought under French colours, but were probably manned by the debased of all nations. I can form no idea how many were killed or wounded on board the gunboats, but from the great number of men on board, and from the length of the action, there must have been great slaughter; neither can I say positively how long the engagement lasted, but I should think, at least, from three to four hours. To the chief mate, too much credit cannot be given, for saving the ship after the captain was shot.

I understood from Captain Crocker that he received the amount of his cargo of tobacco and staves in *doubloons*, that his intention was to proceed with this money to Alicant, to purchase a cargo of brandy and wine for the New York market, and that he had written to a merchant in Alicant, some weeks previous to our leaving Gibraltar, to have their wine and brandy ready to take on board immediately on our arrival, at a price already agreed upon. Accordingly about the middle of August, after lying twenty days in Gibraltar, we sailed for Alicant. The poor sick man before mentioned grew worse and worse, with little or no prospect of recovery. I think our captain made a great mistake in not leaving the poor fellow in the hospital at Gibraltar, where he would have been better attended and suffered less than he did in a small confined forecastle, deprived of medical aid and suitable nourishment.

On our arrival at Alicant, after a passage of ten days, he was a mere skeleton and very near to death. When the health boat came along side to visit the vessel and saw this man bolstered up on deck, they were afraid to come on board, and immediately ordered the captain to proceed to the quarantine ground forthwith, and to have no communication with the shore, or with any vessel or boat, without a permit from the health officer. The quarantine ground was about a mile to the eastward of the harbour, and about half a mile from the shore. Here we lay for more than a month, when the sick man died, and we were allowed to bury him in the sand just above high-water mark. He had no contagious disease, but gradually wasted away; his leg mortified, and the poor fellow's suffering was so severe, that it was a relief to see him die.

We were not allowed to take on board our cargo in the ordinary way, from lighters, but, as follows: some fifty or sixty pipes of brandy and wine were fastened together and towed in the water near our vessel, where they were left for our boat to tow them alongside, and for us to hoist them on board and stow them away with our small and weak crew; in this manner we took on board all our cargo. Whenever we got any fresh provisions or fruit from the town, it was sent off in a boat, to a considerable distance from the vessel, and then put on board of our boat. They appeared to avoid all direct communication with us as though we had the plague on board.

Thus we received our cargo, and paid for it in *doubloons* without the privilege of going on shore; and during our long stay here, neither the captain nor any other person belonging to our vessel ever put foot on shore, except when at one time the mate and four seamen were allowed to land on the sand-beach, just long enough to bury the dead man, during which time they were closely watched by the officers of the government.

We were all happy when the day arrived to sail once more for our native land, which was, as near as I can recollect, about the first of October, 1800. Some days after leaving this port, while sailing gently down the Mediterranean with a light breeze, we fell in with a small lateen-rigged privateer, under French colours, mounting four guns, and, I should think, manned by about fifty of the worst and most ferocious looking fellows I ever saw, all armed with pistols and long knives. They boarded us in their own boat, and, to our surprise, the captain appeared a mild, gentlemanly man. Neither he nor his men would speak to us in English, they affected not to understand our language; but through one of the men, who spoke a little broken English, the captain gave us to understand that he wanted a pipe of brandy and a pipe of wine for stores, and would give our captain an order on the owner of his privateer (whom he represented to be a respectable merchant residing in Marseilles), for the amount of the wine and brandy, and that he would pay the money at sight of this order. Our captain, being greatly agitated, was glad to comply with the request for the brandy and wine, without, for a moment, questioning the validity of the order, and took his draft, without scanning its contents, happy to get clear of such a cut-throat looking set of rascals. We were not quite easy, being somewhat in fear of a second visit from this gentlemanly captain, until he was fairly out of sight.

On our way down the Straits we touched at Gibraltar for water, stores, &c. Here the captain (being unable to read French himself), got his order translated. It proved to be only *jeu d'esprit* or hoax of this polite sea-robber. We remained but a few days at Gibraltar, only long enough to fill up our water and take on board sea-stores, &c, when we again sailed for New York. During the whole of this homeward passage, I do not recollect one circumstance worth recording.

We arrived in New York about the middle of November, when we were all paid, off and discharged. I here learned, with grief and pain, that my honoured father was no more. He had been dead about three weeks on our arrival; his death was a sad blow indeed to all his family and friends; he was a kind, affectionate husband, a tender father, and a generous friend. To me it was an irreparable loss; I had lost my stay and guide, the only male friend, capable of directing my future course. In short, I was cast upon the wide world, to make my way without fortune and without friends.

My mother's health at this time was very delicate, and she was now left, bereaved of her husband, with little or no, means of sustaining and supporting herself and three young boys, aged from three to seven years.

I returned home to comfort her, and to mingle our tears of grief together. My two eldest brothers being absent, I was at this time a great solace to my distressed and widowed mother. I remained however but a few months at home, before I found it absolutely necessary to seek employment.

CHAPTER 2

Voyage in the Schooner *Industry*

On the 1st of November, 1805, I shipped with Captain James Kennedy, onboard the schooner *Industry*, as chief mate, to perform a voyage to the island of Tenerife. On the 18th of the same month, we commenced loading with Indian corn, flour, stores, etc. The *Industry* was a good vessel, nearly new, burden 150 tons; and was owned by Messrs. Le Roy, Bayard & McEvers, of New York. We finished loading in about a week, and sailed from New York on the 24th of October, bound for Santa Cruz, Tenerife.

Nothing occurred worth noticing on this passage until we made the Island of Madeira, on the 27th of December; thirty-one days from New York. At noon this day we took our departure from this island. It then bore N. N. W., distant twelve leagues, and with a strong gale at N. W. we ran down for Tenerife. There are two small islands called the Salvages, which lie almost directly in the track. They are quite low, and in a dark night can be seen but a very short distance. Our captain judged we should be down in the neighbourhood of them about 2 o'clock, a. m.

It being my first watch on deck, namely, from 8 o'clock till midnight, the captain gave me charge of the deck, telling me to call him at midnight, and saying that he would shorten sail at 2 o'clock, and if the wind continued strong it would be better to lie by until daylight. He then went below, and in a few minutes was sound asleep.

I accordingly carried as much sail as the schooner would bear, until midnight, when I called Captain Kennedy, told him it was blowing very strong, and that it was necessary to shorten sail, as we were no doubt drawing near the Salvages. He appeared to rouse up a little, and then sank into a sound sleep. I returned to the deck and waited some minutes, when I again called, and endeavoured by repeated shakings and loud calls to arouse him; but all to no purpose. I could not awaken him and was therefore obliged to go on deck and shorten sail. At 2 a. m., I hove the schooner to, determined to lie by till daylight. I then went below, giving the watch on deck orders to call me at the first dawn of day. This order was obeyed, and when I came on deck the Salvages were about a mile distant on our lee beam, with a terrible surf breaking and dashing the white foam high in the air with a terrific roar. We immediately made sail and passed quite near the largest of these desolate and barren looking islands, which are, I should judge, about a mile asunder, with a bad reef extending from the larger to the smaller.

I was now enabled to get the captain on deck and show him the danger we had escaped. Captain Kennedy was a kind, amiable man, and always treated me with respect and kindness—but truth compels me to add, that he was the most profound sleeper I ever knew, and I verily believe, that if a two-and-forty pounder had been fired off on deck, directly over his head, it would not have awaked him, or disturbed his slumbers.

The next day we made the island of Tenerife, and got safe to anchor in the port of Santa Cruz on the 29th of Dec, after a boisterous passage of thirty-three days. We were this day visited by the health boat, and, though all well, were ordered to perform quarantine for four days, after which time we got *pratique* and commenced discharging our cargo, which was taken on shore in small lighters.

We found lying at anchor in this port but few vessels, say about half a dozen; three American brigs and schooners, a few small craft belonging to the island, and a large Scotch brig, nearly new, of about 250 tons burden. This brig was from Newfoundland, laden with codfish, bound to London, and was taken in the chops of the English Channel by a French fleet of men-of-war on their passage to the West Indies a few days out from Ro-chefort, and was sent into this port where she was condemned and lay moored, with four bower anchors, topmast and yards on deck, prepared to brave the winter gales, which often blow here with great violence.

About the last of December, 1805, a French brig-of-war touched here for a few days and brought the news of a great naval battle having been fought on the 21st of last October, be-tween the combined fleets of France and Spain, off Cadiz and Trafalgar, and an English fleet under the command of Admiral Lord Nelson; and that Lord Nelson was killed in the action. This was about all the news we heard on this subject for many months.

On referring to the life of Lord Nelson, I find that on the 22nd of July, 1797, he arrived at this port with a British fleet of four line-of-battle ships, and three frigates, and that two days after, at midnight, he manned all the boats of the squadron and attempted to land on the quay and take the town by storm, but was repulsed with great slaughter, and the commander, Admiral Nelson, lost his right arm.

We had discharged about half our cargo when on the 8th of January, about noon, it commenced blowing a gale from the eastward directly on shore. At 3 o'clock p. m. I received a note from Captain Kennedy, requesting me to clear the decks and get ready as soon as possible to go to sea, and stating that he would be on board in the course of an hour or two. I accord-ingly cleared the decks, reefed the sails, and got buoys ready. At 6 o'clock, just an hour before dark, the captain came on board, when we slipped our cables and got under way, and had just time before dark to clear the port.

In the early part of this day a ship arrived off the harbour. The captain went on shore to try the market, ordering the mate to stand off and on, until further orders. We stood off from the land, and just before dark saw the ship and supposed she was at a great distance in the offing, and therefore concluded we were several miles asunder.

At 8 p. m. it became very dark, and blew a strong gale from the S. E. and E. S. E. directly on shore, attended with rain and much thunder and lightning, but as we had got everything snug, and judged ourselves about five miles from the land, we felt quite safe. Just then the steward called the captain and myself to supper. Captain Kennedy told me I had better go below, and that he would keep a look-out, and take a little tea and biscuit on deck. I had entered the cabin when I felt a terrible shock. I ran to the companion-way, when I saw a ship athwart our bows. At that moment our foremast went by the board, carrying with it our main-topmast. In an instant the two vessels separated, and we were left a perfect wreck. The ship showed a light for a few moments and then disappeared, leaving us to our fate. When we came to examine our situation, we found our bowsprit gone close to the night-heads.

The foremast in its fall had crushed and broken the cook-house, lee gunwale, and waist-boards. The main-topmast in its fall tore the mainsail to pieces; and the mainmast, thus left without support, was surging and springing in such a manner that we feared every moment it would go also. The gale increased, and blew with great violence directly on shore. To retard the schooner's drift, we kept the wreck of the foremast, bowsprit, sails, spars, &c, fast by the bowsprit shrouds and other ropes, so that we drifted to leeward but about two miles the hour. To secure the mainmast was now the first object. I therefore took with me one of the best of the crew and carried the end of a rope cable with us up to the mainmast head, and clenched it round the mast while it was badly springing. We then took the cable to the windlass and hove taught, and thus effectually secured the mast. It was now 10 o'clock at night, and we could do no more for the present, I then gave the charge of the deck to one of our best men, with orders to keep a good look-out and call me if there should be any change of wind or weather. We were then drifting directly on shore where the cliffs were rocky, abrupt, and almost perpendicular, and were perhaps 1000 feet high. At each flash of lightning we could see the surf break, whilst we heard the awful roar of the sea dashing and breaking against the rocks and caverns of this iron-bound island.

When I went below, I found the captain in the act of going to bed; and as near as I can recollect, the following dialogue took place:

"Well, Captain Kennedy, what shall we do next? we have now about six hours to pass before daylight, and, according to my calculation, we have only about three hours more drift; still, before that time there may, perhaps, be some favourable change."

He answered, "Mr. Coggeshall, we have done all we can, and can do nothing more; I am resigned to my fate, and think nothing can save us."

I replied, "Perhaps you are right; still, I am resolved to struggle to the last. I am too young to die; I am only twenty-one years of age, and have a widowed mother, three brothers, and a sister, looking to me for support and sympathy. No, sir, I will struggle and persevere to the last."

"Ah!" said he, "What can you do? Our boat will not live five minutes in the surf, and you have no other resource."

"I will take the boat," said I, "and when she fills, I will cling to a spar, I will not die until my strength is exhausted, and I can breathe no longer."

Here the conversation ended, when the captain covered his head with a blanket. I then wrote the substance of our misfortune in the log-book, and also a letter to my mother, rolled them up in a piece of tarred canvas, and, assisted by the carpenter, put the package into a tight keg; thinking that this might probably be thrown on shore, and thus our friends might perhaps know of our end. I then went on deck to take another look at our perilous situation. The night was excessively dark, the wind was blowing a terrible gale, directly on shore, with a high rolling sea at short intervals, we had awful peals of thunder, and sharp vivid lightning: every bright flash revealed to us more clearly our impending danger, and as we were momentarily drifting nearer to the lofty cliffs, the surf seemed to break and roar with increased fury.

At this critical moment, when all human aid was impo-

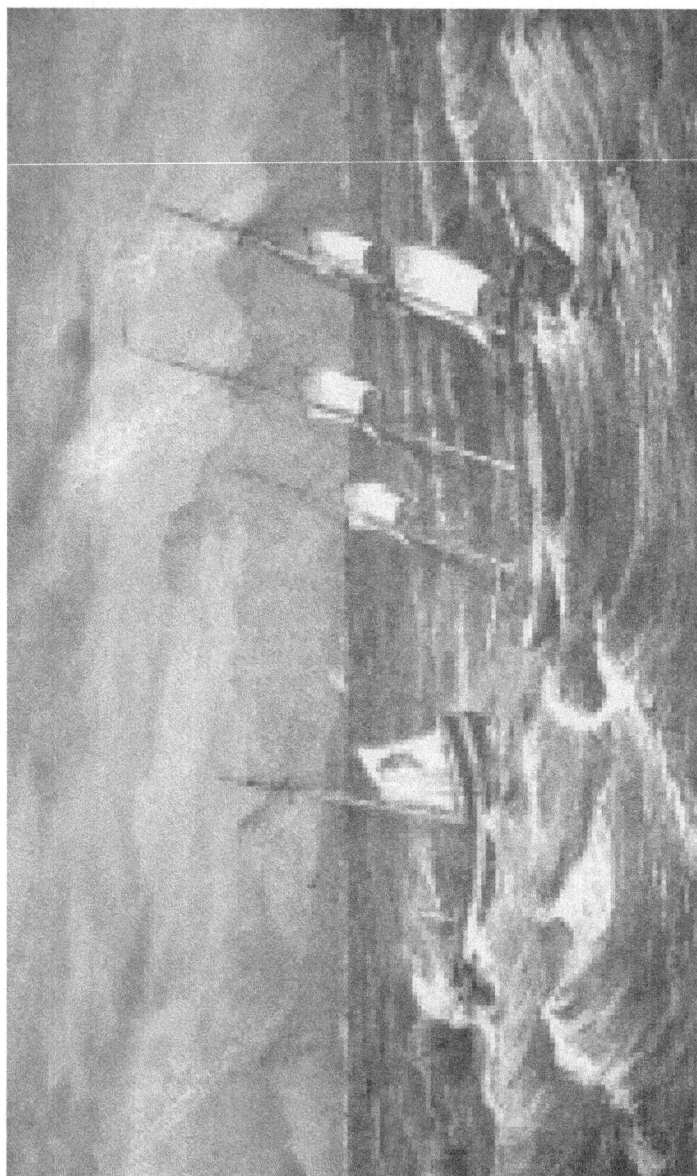

SCHOONER *INDUSTRY* AND SHIP *CATHERINE*, 8TH JAN. 1806

tent and unavailing, a kind Providence came to our relief, and snatched us from a watery grave; for at midnight, one hour after this trying scene, the gale gradually died away until it became quite calm. At 2 o'clock in the morning a light breeze sprung up, from off the land, and we were saved. With the little land breeze, and a favourable current setting along shore to the southward, the schooner was gently swept off and along the south end of the island. At early dawn, *viz*: at 3 o'clock, I called all hands, and now our captain acted like a man. Having been in early life bred a carpenter, he could use tools adroitly, and we all set to work in good earnest.

We had a new mainsail and jib below, which we instantly bent, and rigged out a square-sail boom for a bowsprit, and in an hour our vessel was completely rigged into a sloop, and we were slowly steering off shore.

At broad daylight we were about a mile off the land. Santa Cruz was entirely out of sight, and not a ship or boat to be seen. We gradually drifted with the wind and current to the southward of the island. The winds continued light, and the weather fine, for several days; in the mean time we rigged a small jury-mast with a spare topmast, and set as many jibs as we could muster, daily beating against the wind and current, until at the end of eighteen days we again reached Santa Cruz, and regained our former anchorage.

At the sight of our vessel, the whole town was astonished, as we had been given up for lost, and both vessel and cargo had been abandoned to the underwriters in New York. The ship that ran us down, proved to be the *Catharine,* Captain George Dowdall, of New York. Their report was, that they saw nothing of the schooner after the two vessels separated, and concluded, of course, that we immediately sank, and that every soul had perished. I understood that the *Catharine* received considerable injury about the bows, and lost a bower anchor and sixty or seventy fathoms of cable.

There was an American brig here belonging to Bath (then in the province of Maine), to sail the next day, so that we were enabled to write to our friends that we were still among the living. When our captain went on shore at Santa Cruz, he was treated with great kindness and hospitality by all the principal merchants of the town, and we were all looked upon as so many men risen from the dead.

We soon discharged the remainder of our cargo, and had several surveys of the vessel; and as no suitable spars could be found there to make a new foremast and bowsprit, the schooner was condemned and sold at public auction, for the benefit of the underwriters.

Captain Kennedy then purchased the Scotch prize brig, to which myself and all the crew of the *Industry* were transferred. I do not recollect the Scotch name of this vessel, but Captain Kennedy called her the *Jane Kennedy* after one of his daughters.

We took on board a quantity of stone ballast, sea stores, &c, &c, and on the 6th of March sailed for New York. We had contrary winds and calms a great part of the passage, and on the 26th of April, 1806, after a long and tedious passage of forty-nine days, arrived off Sandy Hook. While standing in near the Hook, I saw a gun fired from the British ship of war *Leander* at a small sloop, standing in shore. I saw the sloop heave to, but did not know at that time that the shot struck her. When we got to New York, I heard that a man by the name of John Pierce was killed. The next morning I went on board the sloop, lying at the wharf. The shot had struck the taffrail, shivered it in pieces, and one of the splinters killed Pierce, while standing at the helm. The death of this man, occurring at the entrance of the port, and in our own waters, while we were at peace with England, caused a great excitement against the perpetrators of this outrage, and the whole country felt that it was an insult to the nation, and called aloud for redress.

A day or two after our arrival, the crew of our vessel were discharged and paid off, Captain Kennedy retaining his apprentice boy and myself; and after getting the brig calked and painted she was laid up, until Captain Kennedy could hear from Scotland, where he had written to her former owners, offering to sell her to them at a fair valuation, they having the privilege of obtaining a new register, &c. She was, of course, worth more to them than to others. Captain Kennedy purchased this vessel without any papers, and came home with a simple certificate from the American Consul at Tenerife, that he had purchased and paid for the brig at Santa Cruz.

The brig being now in perfect order, I got leave of absence to visit my mother, in Connecticut, and as Captain Kennedy had no further need of my services, we separated with mutual good wishes for our future prosperity.

CHAPTER 3

Voyage and a Short Cruise in the Letter-of-Marque Schooner

David Porter

All the ships belonging to Messrs. A. Gracie & Sons being now laid up, they had at the time no further occasion for my services, which I did not regret, not from any want of regard for my employers, who were good, just, and liberal men, but I was glad to go into some other business. I had serious doubts about the propriety and justice of supplying the British with bread-stuffs and provisions while my country was at war with that nation. It is true, I had made the last two voyages to Lisbon in the same business, but was never quite satisfied that it was right, and I was glad of an opportunity to leave the trade.

At this period of the war, there were but three ways for captains of merchant ships to find employment in their vocation, namely, to enter the United States Navy as sailing-masters, to go privateering, or to command a letter-of-marque, carry a cargo, and as it were force trade, and fight their way or run, as the case might be; and, as an alternative, I chose that of a letter-of-*marque*. I gave myself some weeks leisure, and then consulted a few friends on the subject of purchasing a pilot-boat schooner, and going into the French trade. After looking about for a suitable vessel, I at length met with a fine schooner of about 200 tons burden, called the *David Porter*. She was built in Milford, my native town, and had made but one voyage, which was from

New York to St. Jean de Luz, France, thence to St. Bartholomew, and from that place to Providence, R. I., where she then lay. She was a fine fast-sailing vessel, and tolerably well armed, having a long 18-pounder on a pivot amidships, four 6-pounders, with muskets, pistols, &c. I purchased one-half of this schooner for $6000, from the former owners in Milford, Connecticut. They retained the other half for their own account. My New York friends, Messrs. Lawrence & Whitney, and James Lovett, Esq., bought one quarter, and I retained the other quarter for my own account.

We decided on a voyage, from Providence to Charleston, S. C, and thence to France. I arrived at Providence on the 21st of October, 1813. Here I purchased 1500 bushels of salt at 65 cents per bushel, from Messrs. Archibald Gracie & Sons, and after getting the salt on board, filled up the vessel with sundry articles of Northern produce; the whole cargo amounted to $3,500. I took with me, as first lieutenant, my former mate in the Canton, Mr. Samuel Nichols, Joseph Anthony second, and Charles Coggeshall third lieutenant, with a company of about thirty petty officers and men. My boatswain, carpenter, and gunner, with several of the crew, had just been discharged from the frigate *President,* and were very efficient, good men.

I left Providence on the 10th of November, with a fine fresh gale from the N. N. W., and in a few hours ran down to Newport, there to lie a few days, to get ready for sea, and to wait a favourable time to go out of the harbour. To do that I required a dark night, and a N. E. snow-storm; for in those days, to evade the vigilance of the enemy, we were obliged to wait for such nights to leave or enter our ports. On the morning of the 14th, I met with a New York friend, Mr. A. Foster, and to this gentleman I committed what little treasure I had left after getting ready for sea. The whole consisted of thirty guineas, sundry bank notes, and my gold watch. I requested that he would stop at Stamford, Connecticut, on his way to New York, and leave them with my sister, Miss H. C.

Mr. Foster kindly executed this little commission, and is entitled to my best thanks.

At this time there was a British 74 and a frigate cruising off the harbour of Newport, to blockade the port and watch the movements of the U. S. frigate *President,* which ship was then lying at Providence.

Towards evening, on the 14th of November, I got under way, with the wind at E. N. E. No vessel was permitted to go to sea without first presenting a clearance to the commanding officer at the outer fort, at the entrance of the harbour; consequently, I ran down near the fort just before dark, and, for fear of any mistake or detention, took my papers and went myself to the commanding officer, and got permission to pass by showing a light in the main shrouds for a few minutes. It soon commenced snowing, with a fresh gale at N. E. We ran rapidly out of the harbour, and got outside of the blockading squadron. My greatest fear now was of running on to Block Island. Fortunately, however, at daylight we saw no land, neither was there a single sail in sight.

On the 17th of November, in lat. 36° 4' N., long, about 73° W., was chased by a man-of-war brig. He being to windward, I bore off, and soon had the pleasure to run him out of sight. On the 24th, off Georgetown, was chased all day by a man-of-war brig, with a schooner in company. They being to leeward, I consequently tacked and plied to windward, and made good my retreat before night, I could have got into Georgetown the next day, but fearing my cargo would not sell as well as at Charleston, I stood on for that port.

November the 26th, at 6 o'clock, daylight, in ten fathoms water, off Cape Roman, saw a man-of-war brig on our weather quarter, distant about three miles. He soon made sail in chase. I kept wide off to leeward in hopes of drawing him down, so that I could weather him on the opposite tack. This manoeuvre did not succeed, as the enemy only kept off about four points. We both therefore maintained our relative positions, and the chase continued for four hours. I had determined not to run to leeward, for fear of coming in contact with another foe, but to hug the wind and run in shore. At 10 o'clock a. m. saw Charleston lighthouse, bearing north, about ten miles distant. I set my ensign, and hauled close to the wind; this brought the enemy on my starboard beam, at long gunshot distance. I then fired my centre gun, but could not quite reach him, the wind being light from the northward. At half-past ten I gave him another shot, and though it did not take effect, with a spy-glass I saw the shot dash the water on his quarter. I suppose the reason he did not fire was, that he could not reach us with his carronades. At 11 *ditto*, when within five miles of Charleston Bar, I saw two schooners coming over the bar, and bearing directly down upon the brig, when he squared his yards and ran away to leeward.

The two schooners were the famous privateer *Decatur,* of Charleston, with seven guns, and a complement of over a hundred men, and the other schooner was the letter-of-marque *Adeline,* Captain Craycroft, of Philadelphia, bound to France. The schooners took no notice of the brig, hauled to the eastward, and were quickly out of sight. I soon crossed the bar; and got up to Charleston without any further difficulty, and there learned that the man-of-war brig was the *Dotterall,* carrying 18 guns

It will doubtless be recollected by all those who are familiar with our late war with England, that the privateer *Decatur,* Captain D. Diron, captured, a few months before this period, his B. M. schooner *Dominico.* The following is the official account of the action:

(Copy.)

Charleston, August 21st, 1813.
Sir:—I have the honour to inform you that the privateer schooner *Decatur,* Captain Dominique Diron, of this port, arrived here yesterday with His B. M. schooner *Dominico* her prize. She was captured on the 5th inst. after a most gallant and desperate action of one hour, and carried by boarding; having all her officers killed or wounded except one midshipman. The *Dominico* mounted fifteen guns, one 32-pounder on a pivot, and had a complement of 83 men at the commencement of the action, sixty of whom were

killed or wounded. She was one of the best equipped and manned vessels of her class I have ever seen. The *Decatur* mounted seven guns, and had a complement of 103 men at the commencement of the action, nineteen of whom were killed and wounded. I have the honour to be, with great respect, your most obedient servant,

John H. Dent.

Hon. Wm. Jones, Secretary of the Navy.

During the combat, which lasted an hour, the King's packet-ship *Princess Charlotte* remained a silent spectator of the scene, and as soon as the vessels were disengaged from each other she tacked about and stood to the southward. She had sailed from St. Thomas, bound to England, under convoy, to a certain latitude, of the *Dominico*. The loss on board the *Dominico* consisted of killed thirteen, wounded forty-seven, five of whom mortally.

On my arrival at Charleston, I appointed Mr. John Marshall our consignee and commercial agent. We disposed of most of our cargo at a good profit, the salt at $1.50 per bushel, and the other articles at like good rates.

After disposing of my cargo, I found no difficulty in obtaining a freight for France; but before I could commence taking in my cotton, I was obliged to purchase about twenty-five tons of pig-iron at $65 per ton, and some other small iron ballast. The whole amounted to $1700; but it was indispensable, and I could not take a cargo of cotton safely without it. My whole cargo consisted of 331 bales of compressed cotton, and sixteen kegs of potash: 209 of these bales I took on freight at 26 cents per pound, and five *per cent*, primage. The whole amount of my freight was $14,717, exclusive of the 122 bales belonging to the owners of the vessel. Allowing the owners to pay the same proportion or rate of freight as the other shippers, the schooner would have made a gross freight of about $23,300, which was certainly a great price for carrying 331 bales of cotton to France. For the 122 bales purchased for owners' account, I paid fourteen cents per pound: a more ordinary quality could have been bought for twelve to thirteen cents. About forty bales of the cotton, belonging to the owners, I carried on deck. It certainly appears like an enormous freight to make $23,000 in a small schooner of only 200 tons; but when the expense of sailing one of these letter-of-marques is taken into consideration, it is not so great as might at first appear. The insurance at this time out to France, was from fifteen to twenty *per cent.*—seamen's wages $30 per month—and other expenses in like proportion.

On the 16th of December I finished loading, and got all the crew on board, and the next day was ready for sea, but unfortunately the wind blew fresh from the southward, with dark, disagreeable, rainy weather.

The Congress of the United States had lately assembled at Washington, and great fears were entertained by many that an embargo would soon be laid. I was, of course, extremely anxious to get out of port, as such a measure would have been ruinous to myself and the other owners of my vessel; and as it was impossible to get over the bar while the wind was blowing strong, directly into the harbour, I therefore, to avoid being stopped, and to keep my men on board, judged it best to drop as low down the harbour as possible and watch the first favourable moment to proceed to sea. Fortunately the weather cleared up the next day, and with a favourable breeze and fine weather, I left the port of Charleston on the 20th of December, 1813, bound to Bordeaux. I had a good run off the coast, and met with nothing worth remarking until the 27th, about a week after leaving port, when I fell in with a small English brig from Jamaica, bound to Nova Scotia.

As it was about four o'clock in the afternoon, and at the time blowing a strong gale from the N.W. with a high sea running, I did not think it safe to board him until the gale should moderate and the sea become smoother, and therefore ordered him to carry as much sail as possible, and follow me on our course to the eastward until better weather. He reluctantly followed, and once before dark I was obliged to hail and give him to understand that if he showed too great a disposition to lag behind, or did not carry all the sail his brig could bear, he would feel the effect of one of my stern guns. This threat had the desired effect, and he followed kindly at a convenient distance until midnight, when it became very dark and squally, and we soon after lost sight of our first prize, which I did not much regret, as I could not conveniently spare men enough to send him into port.

From this time until we got near the European coast we scarcely saw a sail, and did not meet with a single man-of-war. Thus, while the whole coast of the United States was literally lined with English cruisers, on the broad ocean there were very few to be seen: a clear proof that the risk of capture between Newport and Charleston, was infinitely greater than in going to France.

At this period, we were not obliged to deliver the goods on freight at any particular place, but at any port in France, from St. Jean-de-Luz to Ostend. My bills of lading were filled up upon this principle, to Bordeaux, or a port in France, so that on the arrival of the goods, the owners or agents were bound to receive them at any place where the vessel was fortunate enough to enter. My object was to get as near Bordeaux as possible; still I did not like to attempt entering the Garonne, as the English generally kept several frigates and smaller vessels stationed directly off the Cordovan Light, which rendered it extremely difficult and hazardous. I therefore decided to run for the harbour of La Teste.

About a week before we got into port, while in the Bay of Biscay, namely on the 19th and 20th of January, we encountered one of the most severe gales from the westward that I ever experienced. It commenced early on the morning of the 19th, and blew a perfect hurricane, which soon raised a high cross-sea. At 8 o'clock a. m. I hove the schooner to under a double-reefed foresail, lowered the fore-yard near the deck, and got everything as snug as possible. At 12 o'clock, noon, a tremendous sea struck her in the wake of the starboard fore-shrouds. The force of the sea broke one of the top timbers or stanchions, and split open the plank-sheer so that I could see directly into the hold.

The violence of the blow and the weight of water that came

on board threw the vessel nearly on her beam ends. Fortunately the foresail was split and the bulwarks, torn away by the water, and being thus relieved she gradually righted. We then threw overboard two of the lee guns, water-casks. &c, and after nailing tarred canvas and leather over the broken plank-sheer got ready to veer ship, fearing the injury received in the wake of the starboard fore-shrouds would endanger the foremast. We accordingly got ready to hoist a small piece of the mainsail, and then kept her off before the wind for a few minutes, and watched a favourable, smooth time to bring her to the wind on the other tack.

During the time that the schooner ran before the wind, she appeared literally to leap from one sea to another. We soon, however, brought her up to the wind on the other tack without accident; and thus under a small piece of the mainsail, she lay to pretty well. But as the gale continued to rage violently, I feared we might ship another sea. and therefore prepared, as it were, to anchor the vessel head to wind. For this purpose we took a square-sail-boom, spanned it at each end with a new four-inch rope, and made our small bower cable fast to the bight of the span, and with the other end fastened to the foremast, threw it overboard, and payed out about sixty fathoms of cable; she then rode like a gull on the water, and I was absolutely astonished to see the good effect of this experiment. The spar broke the sea, and kept the schooner nearly head to the wind until the gale subsided.

The next day, in the afternoon, January the 20th, we again made sail, and on the 26th, six days after this tempest, got safe into La Teste, thirty-seven days from Charleston. While we providentially escaped destruction, other ships were less fortunate; many vessels were stranded and wrecked along the coast; five sail of English transports were thrown on shore near La Teste, and most of their crews perished in the same gale. On my arrival at La Teste, all my papers were sent up to Paris, and although we were all well, still we were compelled by the government to ride quarantine for six days.

La Teste is a poor little village, principally supported by fish

SCHOONER *DAVID PORTER* LYING IN THE BAY OF BISCAY JAN 30TH 1814

and oysters taken in its waters, and sold in Bordeaux, from which city it is distant thirty miles, and fifty-four from the mouth of the Garonne. The harbour has a bad sand-bar at its mouth; is fit entrance only for small vessels of a light draft of water; and even for them it is dangerous to approach in bad weather.

I will here insert a copy of the first letter written to my owners on my arrival on the 9th of February, 1814.

Messrs. Lawrence and Whitney, James Lovett, Esq., and the other owners of the schooner:

Gentlemen:—I arrived here on the 20th of last month, after a rough passage of thirty-seven days. No sale at all can be had for cotton, and no security for anything; the agents and owners of the cotton are unwilling to receive it, and one and all refuse to pay the freight. As soon as I can obtain permission, I shall discharge the vessel, and forward the cargo all up to Bordeaux by land, and endeavour to force by law the consignees of the cotton to receive it and pay the freight. In fine, I shall be happy if they do not throw the cotton on my hands for the freight.

No merchant in Bordeaux is willing to advance me half the amount of the freight due and retain it as security. In short, it is with the greatest difficulty that I can obtain sufficient money from my consignees, Messrs. Brun *frères*, to pay the necessary disbursements on my vessel. It is therefore at present impossible for me to say what I shall do. If I could collect my freight, I could remit the amount to the United States through England, and gain on the exchange from seventeen to twenty *per cent.*: or if I could get enough advanced on my cotton to purchase part of a cargo of wine and brandy, and return to some port in the United States or the West Indies, I could perhaps pick up the residue of a cargo from the enemy on the broad ocean.

As I am now situated, I know not what to do. Should I send my vessel home by my first officer, and should he be captured on the way, you would perhaps blame me, and say, 'Why did he not come home in the vessel himself?' To leave the freight and cargo here in the hands of strangers, I cannot, and dispose of the cotton at a ruinous sacrifice, I will not; and, on the other hand, to keep the vessel here upon expense is very painful; and thus the whole business is beset with difficulties on every side. You may however rely upon my best exertions to promote your interest, and come what will, you may rest assured, gentlemen, that I shall act from pure motives, and strive to do justice to the utmost of my abilities.

After performing six days quarantine, I proceeded on horseback to Bordeaux. The road being intricate and somewhat difficult, I hired a guide to accompany me the greater part of the way. We often had to pass over barren sands and through pine forests. My guide was a merry fellow. He was mounted on stilts about two feet high, and with a long balance-pole, and a musket slung over his shoulder, had no difficulty in keeping up with my horse, travelling at the rate of five or six miles an hour. We passed through several small towns and villages on the way, but none of much note. I found the inhabitants civil and kind, but poor and ignorant. The inns and stopping-places were dirty and comfortless; and after an unpleasant jaunt of six hours we arrived at Bordeaux. Here I made an arrangement with the house of Messrs. Brun *frères*, to transact my business in this place, and to direct me how to proceed with respect to landing my cargo at La Teste. I remained at Bordeaux two days, and after having settled on a plan with respect to landing and storing my cargo, I returned again to La Teste, and as there was no public conveyance, was compelled to return on horseback.

From Messrs. Brun *frères* I took a letter to Madame Caupos, a widow lady, whose husband had been a merchant, and after his death, she continued to transact nearly all the commercial business of the place. She was a polite, well educated, and a person of excellent character. To this lady I consigned my vessel and cargo, so far as it respected La Teste, and agreed with her to attend to the landing, weighing, storing, and forwarding of my cotton to

Bordeaux. She owned two large warehouses and had every facility and convenience for storing my whole cargo; and with one young man as clerk, performed the whole business to my entire satisfaction. In fine, she was the only person in the town capable of receiving and forwarding my cargo to Bordeaux.

Though La Teste was a poor little town, and without much trade, yet there were there several polite, agreeable, and well-bred families; and although the port was difficult of ingress and egress on account of a dangerous bar, within the harbour it was quite safe from all winds.

After several days' detention, waiting permits from Bordeaux, bad weather, &c, I at length finished discharging my cargo, and had it all safely stored on the 15th of February, but on account of the bad state of the roads, and the difficulty of obtaining carts, I was unable to get. the cotton up to Bordeaux. France, was now in a very unsettled state, threatened by its enemies on every side. It was reported, while I was there, that a part of the Russian and Austrian armies were within thirty leagues of Paris, and that Lord Wellington with his army was in the Landes in pursuit of Marshal Soult, who was on his way to Toulouse, and great fears were entertained that a part of the English army would soon be in Bordeaux. I was therefore extremely anxious to get away at all hazards, not knowing whether the English would respect private persons and private property.

In this state of things I wrote to my owners on the 7th March, 1814. The following is an extract from my letter:—

I have this day returned from La Teste, where I have been staying the last week, getting my vessel ready for sea. I have at length prevailed on Messrs. Brun *frères* to advance me money enough to pay my disbursements, and also to furnish me with sufficient means to purchase hundred casks of wine, and fifty pipes of brandy. I have chartered a small vessel to transport the wine and brandy from this place to La Teste, and got it insured here against all risks, for seven *per cent*, premium. I hope the *chasse marée*, with the wine and brandy, will arrive safe at La Teste the day after tomorrow, when I shall return to that place and send the schooner off to New York, as soon as possible, under command of my first officer, Mr. Samuel Nichols.

We are all in hubbub and confusion here, and threatened on all sides by the enemy. All my cargo is still lying in store at La Teste, except about twenty bales of cotton, which are here in the hands of Messrs. Brun *frères*.

I have had considerable trouble and anxiety since I arrived here, and have been obliged to make frequent journeys on horseback between this place and La Teste, and sometimes am obliged to ride half the night, and take shelter where I can best find it on the road.

All the American vessels have left this place, for fear of the English, and have gone down near the mouth of the Garonne—some are bound home to America, and others will strive to get to La Rochelle, as that is a strongly fortified town, and will probably hold out longer than this place. Every day brings us worse news from Paris and other quarters, and, from present appearances, this country cannot hold out much longer.

The large tract of country lying between Bayonne and Bordeaux is familiarly called the Landes. It is bounded on the west by the Bay of Biscay, and extends about twenty-five leagues east into the interior, and is, I think, the poorest part of France.

The face of the country is generally low, flat, sandy, and barren. Its forests consist principally of pine or fir trees, and the land is, for the most part, miserably cultivated. The peasantry are wretchedly poor, and chiefly clothed in sheepskins. The Basque is the language of the country, and it is only the upper classes, or educated people, who speak French. In the summer season the sands are extremely hot, and in the spring and fall months, the country being low, are often wet and muddy, which, I suppose, is the cause of so many of the country people, particularly the peasants and shepherds, walking on stilts, a foot or two above the ground, with a long balance-pole to support them and regulate their movements. I have seen them in the morning at a distance, when the weather was a little foggy, and they absolutely appeared like giants, walking over the tall grass and small trees. I used frequently to ask them why they preferred walking on stilts. Their answer generally was, to keep their feet dry, remarking also, that they could travel much faster, and with more ease, than with their feet on the ground.

This region is very unlike the other parts of France; and should a stranger visit the Landes, without seeing any other portion of the kingdom, he would naturally conclude that the French nation was only about half civilized. I recollect the first time I landed at La Teste, I was forcibly struck with what I there witnessed.

The pilot who took my vessel into port, came off in a boat rowed (I had almost said manned) by four females; and after the schooner came to anchor, I took one of my sailors with me and returned to the shore, in the pilot's boat. We struck on the sand, where the water was too shallow for the boat to come to the beach, when one of the women immediately jumped into the water, took the huge pilot on her back, and carried him some distance to the dry land. Another female offered to carry me in the same way; to this I would not consent. The sailor, like myself, appeared ashamed to see a female carry a man on her back through the surf, and instantly jumped out and took me on his back to the dry beach. It is true, these women were coarse and rough, but still they were females, and it was therefore impossible for either my sailor or myself so to degrade them. All along the road, from La Teste to Bordeaux, I rarely saw a man at work in the fields; nearly all the labour of cultivating the lands, at that time, was performed by females. Now and then, it is true, I saw an old man, and perhaps a boy, but this did not often occur. All the men, from sixteen to sixty, were pressed into the military service. It was often a melancholy sight, when passing through the towns and villages, to see mere boys forced from their parents, and taken to some military depôt, there to be drilled for a few weeks, and then sent to some of the numerous armies, to be slaughtered like so many sheep and cattle.

Although at this period the Austrian and Russian armies were in the neighbourhood of Paris, and Lord Wellington was at the head of his victorious army overrunning the south of France, it was astonishing to see how little was known to the country people of this region, about the military state of the kingdom. Perhaps not a man in a thousand knew that there was a Russian or an English soldier within a hundred leagues of France.

One day, in passing through a small village, I stopped at a house to get some water, and found a poor woman wringing her hands and weeping, as if her heart would break. On inquiring the cause of her grief, she said, "Sir, they have just taken away my son to join the army, and I have already lost two of my children in the same way. Oh! I shall never see him again!"

I offered the poor, woman all the consolation I could. I told her I was a stranger, and had no right to interfere with the affairs of another nation, but, at the same time, if she would keep quiet, I could assure her that there was no danger of losing her son—that, the wars were nearly at an end, and that peace, in all human probability, would be concluded in a few weeks, when her son would be restored to her again. At these words the poor creature was completely overjoyed, and blessed me a thousand times. When I mounted my horse and rode off, I could not but reflect with indignation on what men call military glory; but, at the next moment, I felt self-reproved, as I, too, commanded an armed vessel, and was, perhaps, going out in a few days to distress the enemies of my country. How strange and inconsistent is poor short-sighted man, condemning others when committing the same offence for which he would denounce his neighbour.

I soon saw that the French ladies and the working women are removed an immeasurable distance from each other, almost as much so as though they did not belong to the same species. I often used to spend a social evening at the hospitable mansion of my consignee, Madame Caupos, and saw there assembled some fifteen or twenty young ladies, and generally not more than three or four gentlemen, and these were military officers who had been wounded and disabled in the wars, and were now here attached to the Custom-House. This was certainly a sad state of society in a national point of view, when there were no young men to marry the fair daughters of France.

Madame Caupos was an amiable, benevolent lady, and deservedly beloved by the whole town; by way of pleasantry, I used often to call her, *La Reine du Village*.

The state of affairs in France daily grew worse and worse. Lord Wellington was following Marshal Soult day after day towards Toulouse. We also received bad news from the North, that the Austrians and Prussians were daily advancing towards Paris, and were then within twenty leagues of that city.

I received on the 5th a letter from Messrs. Brun *frères*, which induced me to hurry up to Bordeaux, to endeavour to bring my business to a better and more decided state, as they were disinclined in consequence of the unsettled state of the country to advance enough for my unavoidable expenses. On the 8th of March I hastened up from La Teste to Bordeaux, to prevent the *chasse-marée* from going round to La Teste, and agreed with the captain and owners of this vessel to proceed with the wine and brandy to La Rochelle as soon as possible.

I then made arrangements with my friends, Messrs. Brun *frères*, and left Bordeaux at 6 o'clock the same evening for La Teste. Soon after leaving the town, I overtook a French gentleman also going to La Teste. He was a military officer, and was engaged on public business, and I found him a most agreeable travelling companion. We rode on, picking our way as well as we could, until it became very dark, when we lost our road, and could find no one to put us in the right path again. After wandering about till two o'clock after midnight, we came to a village, where, after knocking at several houses in vain, we at length found one to which we gained admittance. It was a small house with but two rooms, and not one spare bed, but its inmates were civil and kind. We were cold, wet, and hungry, and they gave us the best they had, which consisted of eggs, bread, and sour wine. Even this was to us a grateful repast. We warmed and sweetened the wine, of which we drank freely, and then lay down on the floor by the fireside till daylight, when we again started for La Teste. We found we had wandered a great distance from the right road, and had still about a league to go before reaching the end of our journey.

On my arrival at La Teste, I lost no time in preparing for sea. There was no other ship or vessel lying here, and no stone ballast, I was therefore compelled to take in sand-ballast in my own boat, and fill up our water casks and take them on board also in my own boat. We had no biscuit on board, and there was but one baker of any consequence in the town. I hastened to this important character, and agreed to take all the bread he could make in two days, and thus, by hurrying and driving, I got ready for sea on the 11th of March. At the end of two days I called on the baker for my supply of bread, when, to my great mortification and disappointment, I could get only loaves enough to fill two bags, and this, for a vessel bound to La Rochelle with a crew of thirty-five in number, was certainly a very small allowance. It is true, I had salt beef and pork enough on board, but no vegetables or rice.

On the 11th in the evening, by letters from Bordeaux, I learned that the day before the town had surrendered by capitulation to a portion of Lord Wellington's army, that no person had been molested, and that perfect good order was observed throughout the city. All this appeared very well with respect to Bordeaux, but still I was fearful that the English would come down and take La Teste before I could get to sea. The next day, March the 12th, the wind was from the westward, and the pilot would not take my vessel to sea. He said that it was impossible to get out; that there was too great a swell on the bar, &c. The next day (the 13th) the weather was clear and the wind fresh at N. N. E. In the morning I prevailed on the pilot to come on board. He told me that the tide would suit at five o'clock in the afternoon, and if there should not be too much sea on the bar at that hour, he would take the vessel out.

Accordingly, at four o'clock I requested him to get under way, and be ready to pass the bar at five. I now found he was unwilling to go out at all. He said, "Captain, if we should succeed in getting out, it would be impossible to land me."

I then offered him double pilotage, told him I was fearful the English would come down in the morning and make a prize of my vessel, and that I would treble his pilotage, and pledge him my honour, that if I waited a week outside, I would land him in safety. At last my patience was exhausted, and I found the more I coaxed and strove to persuade him to go, the more obstinate he became.

At length I said, "If you will not go to sea, pilot, just get the schooner under way and go down below the fort, and anchor there within the bar."

To this proposition he consented. While getting under way, I went below and put into my pocket a loaded pistol, and again returned on deck. We soon got below the fort, and it was five o'clock, precisely the hour he had named as the most suitable to pass out over the bar. I then placed the pistol to his ear, and told him to proceed to sea or he was a dead man, and that if the schooner took the ground his life should pay the forfeit. The poor fellow was terribly frightened, and said he would do his best, and in less than fifteen minutes from the time we filled away, we were fairly over and outside of this formidable bar. I then discharged the pistol, and assured the pilot I would do him no harm, and that I would wait a week if it was necessary, for good weather to land him in safety. He now appeared more tranquil and composed, but would not refrain from talking occasionally of his poor wife and children, and seemed to have a lurking fear that I would carry him to America.

I stood off and on during the night, and in the morning, March 14th, the wind was light off shore from the eastward; as the sea was smooth, I stood close in to the beach, and got our boat ready to land the pilot. I gave him several letters to my friends, and an order on Madame Caupos for a considerable sum over and above his regular pilotage, notwithstanding I had compelled him to take my vessel to sea. At eight o'clock in the morning, my second officer with four men took Mr. Pilot on shore. I gave the officer of the boat positive orders to back the boat stern on to the shore, and let the pilot jump out whenever he could do so with safety. I took a spy-glass, and had the pleasure to see the man land, and scamper up the beach. The boat soon returned and was hoisted on board, when we made sail and stood off in a N.W. direction.

The wind was light from the eastward, and the weather fine and clear. During the night we had not much wind, and of course made but little progress. At daylight, March 15th, 1814, saw a large ship on our weather quarter. I soon made her out to be a frigate, distant about two miles. We were now in a very unpleasant position, early in the morning with a frigate dead to windward. I manoeuvred for some ten or fifteen minutes in hopes of drawing him down to leeward, so that I should be able to weather him on one tack or the other. This was often done at the commencement of the war with American schooners, for if the pilot-boats could succeed in getting the enemy under their lee, they would laugh at their adversary. This manoeuvre however did not succeed, he only kept off four or six points, and I have no doubt he thought it impossible for me to elude his grasp. All this time I was losing ground, and the ship not more than two gun shots to windward.

I held a short consultation with my officers on the subject of attempting to get to windward (which would involve our receiving a broadside), or by running off to leeward. They all thought it best to ply to windward and receive his fire. I stated that we should have to pass him within pistol shot, and the probability was that he would shoot away some of our spars, in which case we should inevitably be captured. I knew the schooner sailed very fast off the wind, and I thought the chance of escape better to run to leeward. I accordingly gave orders to get the square-sail and studding-sails all ready to run up at the same moment; and thus when everything was prepared, the helm was put up and every square-sail set in a moment.

The frigate, not dreaming of my running to leeward, was unprepared to chase off the wind, and I should think it was at least five minutes before he had a studding-sail set: so that I gained about a mile at the commencement of the chase. The wind was light from the E. N. E. and the weather very fine. I ordered holes bored in all the water casks except four, and the water pumped into buckets to wet the sails, also to throw overboard sand ballast to lighten the schooner. After this was done, we began to draw away from the frigate, so that at noon, I had gained about eight or ten miles on the chase. At four in the afternoon he was nearly out of sight, and appeared like a speck on the water. We had now time to look into our own situation, when to my great regret, in lieu of having four casks of water, the carpenter in the confusion had only left two; and as the wind freshened, I found the schooner so light that it was unsafe to haul upon the wind.

Sea-faring men will appreciate what was my unfortunate situation. Thus wide off to sea in the Bay of Biscay, in a light vessel, with scarcely ballast enough to stand upon her bottom, with a crew of thirty-five men, and only two casks of fresh water, and a few loaves of soft bread.

The wind was light during the night, and towards morning it became almost calm. At daylight, to our unspeakable joy, we were in the midst of a small fleet of merchant ships. They had left England under convoy of a frigate and a sloop-of-war, and had separated in a gale of wind a few days before I fell in with them, and were now like a flock of sheep without a shepherd. This little fleet was bound to St. Sebastian, and many of them were loaded with provisions for the British army. The first one I captured was a brig principally laden with provisions. After taking possession, I agreed with the captain that, if he would assist me with his boats and men to transport his cargo from his vessel to my schooner, I would let him go; otherwise I would take what I wanted and destroy his brig. Of course he was glad to make the best of a bad bargain; and thus with the boats of both vessels, in two hours we had provisions enough for a three months' cruise. His cabin was filled with bags of hard biscuit, the staff of life, which we took first, and then got a fine supply of butter, hams, cheese, potatoes, porter, &c, and last, though not least, six casks of fresh water. After this was done, the captain asked me if I would make him a present of the brig and the residue of the cargo, for his own private account, to which I willingly agreed, in consideration of the assistance I had received from him and his men.

I showed him my commission from the Government of the United States, authorizing me to take, burn, sink, or destroy our common enemy, and satisfied him that he was a lawful prize to my vessel. I then gave him a certificate, stating that though his brig was a lawful prize, I voluntarily gave her to him as a present. (This, of course, was only a piece of foolery, but it pleased the captain, and we parted good friends.)

This was on the 16th of March, the day after my escape from the British frigate.

I had now got as much water and provisions as I wanted, and made sail for a ship and two brigs, a mile or two off on our lee beam. Although the wind was very light, I soon took all three of them, and made the same agreement with them as with the other captain, that if they would assist me with all their boats and men to load my schooner with such part of their cargo as best suited me, I would let them go, otherwise I would send them into port as prizes, or destroy their vessels. This was a bitter pill, but they had the choice of two evils, and, of course, complied with my request.

After having taken out a considerable quantity of merchandise, a fresh breeze sprang up from the S. W., and the weather became dark and rainy, which rendered it difficult to continue transporting any more goods from the prizes to our schooner.

At five o'clock in the afternoon, a large ship hove in sight to windward. From aloft, with a spy-glass, I clearly made her out to be the same frigate that had chased me the day before. I recognized her from the circumstance of her having a white jib; all the sails were dark coloured except this jib, which was bleached.

We of course cleared the decks and got ready for another trial of speed, but as my schooner was now in good trim, and night coming on, I had no doubt of dodging him in the dark. He came rapidly down within five or six miles of us, when I ran near my prizes and ordered them all to hoist lanterns. Neither of them up to this time had seen the frigate, and thus, while the lanterns showed their positions, I hauled off silently in the dark. Very soon after this, I heard the frigate firing at his unfortunate countrymen, while we were partaking of an excellent supper at their expense.

The next day, March 17th, it was dark, rainy weather, with strong gales from the S.W.; saw nothing. Stood to the northward, under easy sail, waiting for better weather, to complete loading my little schooner with something valuable from another prize.

I would here remark that small guns, six or nine pounders, are of little or no use on board of small vessels; for if the sea is rough, they cannot be used at all. I have found them of no service, but rather in the way. My only dependence was on my eighteen pounder, mounted amid-ships, on a pivot. This gun I could use in almost any weather. With it and forty small-arms, I found no difficulty in capturing merchant ships. I selected ten of the largest and strongest men I had on board to work the centre gun. One of them was a huge black man, about six feet six inches in height, and large in proportion. To him I gave the command of the gun. Although so powerful a man, he was the best natured fellow in the world, and a general favourite, both with officers and men.

March 18th.—Still a continuation of bad weather, with a strong gale from the westward. At four p. m., saw a frigate and a brig-of-war, off my lee beam, distant about five miles. They made sail in chase, but under my three lower sails, mainsail, fore-sail, and jib, I had no fear of them. I showed my ensign for a few moments, and then plied to windward, making short tacks, and in a few hours they gave up the chase, when I again pursued my course to the northward, under easy sail. Next day, March 19th, the wind moderated, but still there was a very high sea, and very unpleasant weather.

March 20th.—Moderate breezes from the westward, and unpleasant weather. This day I came to the conclusion to land myself somewhere on the coast of France, and to send my vessel home, under the command of my first officer, Mr. Samuel Nichols; and on an examination of a chart of the coast, I concluded to run for Pile Dieu, and land there. Accordingly I shaped my course for the island, and without meeting with any incident worth relating, made the land on the 23rd of March, at four o'clock in the afternoon; at six *ditto* landed on the island in my own boat. It soon became dark, and I was obliged to remain on shore, with my boat's crew, all night. I took with me my clearance and other papers from Bordeaux, with sundry newspapers, and was well received by the Governor and Commissary of Marine.

March 24th.—At six o'clock in the morning, although the weather was thick and rainy, and a strong breeze from the S. W., I sent my boat on board the schooner with a pilot, with orders to get the vessel into the roads, near the town, which is situated on the N. E. end of the island. At two o'clock in the afternoon, the schooner came directly off the town, close in within the fort, where, with our own boat, we took on board six casks of fresh water, some fresh provisions, and sundry small stores. I then obtained liberty from the public authorities to dispatch my vessel to the United States.

At five o'clock in the afternoon of March 24th, 1814, I repaired on board in a shore boat, and after writing a few hasty letters to my friends in the United States, and making a short address to my officers and men, I resigned the command to Mr. Samuel Nichols, and returned on shore with a heavy heart at parting with my little band of brave and faithful followers.

The schooner was soon out of sight, as she stood round the south end of the island. And here I should be doing injustice to the memory of these brave men, did I not give my feeble testimony to their good conduct from the time we left Charleston until parting with them at L'Isle Dieu. I never saw one of them intoxicated in the slightest degree, nor did I ever see one of them ill-treat a prisoner, or attempt to plunder the smallest article. In a word, from the first lieutenant to the smallest boy on board, they were faithful, good, and true men, and to the best of my knowledge and belief, were all born and bred in the United States.

After my schooner sailed, I had leisure to look at the island, which lies in lat. 46° 42' north, long. 2° 27' west. It is five leagues from the continent, directly opposite St. Gilles, and is of a moderate height, about three miles long and one and a half broad. It numbers about two thousand three hundred souls, and is principally supported by the fishing business. It is defended by a pretty strong fort at the mouth of the harbour, with a garrison of about three hundred men. Its produce is not sufficient for its own support; on the contrary, I was told by several of the inhabitants, that it only yields about one quarter part of the breadstuffs that were consumed on the island. It has a snug little harbour, but only accessible to small vessels with a light draft of water. The principal town is rather pleasant, and many of the houses are commodious and well built.

This little island has become interesting from its historical association.

On the first of October, 1795, an English squadron brought here a Bourbon prince and several thousand French emigrants, from England, to join the royal party of La Vendée, and after the fleet of men-of-war and transports had remained here until about the 15th of November, the army debarked at St. Gilles, when the fleet returned to England. [1]

When I landed at L'Isle Dieu, I took with me as one of the boat's crew, the large black man, Philip; I was astonished to see the curiosity expressed here at the sight of a negro. He was followed at every step by a crowd of men, women and children, all desirous to see a black man; and I soon received a pressing message from the Governor's lady to see him. I accordingly took Philip with me and repaired to the residence of the Governor, where were assembled all the first ladies of the island. They had a great many questions to ask about him, respecting the place

1. See Thiers' History French Revolution.

of his birth, whether he was kind and good natured, &c.. When their curiosity was gratified, the fellow begged of me as a favour to be allowed to go on board, as he did not like to be exhibited as a show. This request I readily granted, telling the ladies and gentlemen that I had an Indian on board, and that I would send for him. The Indian came directly on shore, but, to my surprise, there appeared but little curiosity on the part of the inhabitants to see the savage. This island had been as it were shut out from the rest of the world for twenty-five or thirty years, with little or no commerce or communication with other nations, and it is therefore highly probable that very few of its inhabitants had ever seen a negro, and they were of course eager to behold one.

L'Isle Dieu, *March 25th,* 1814. Throughout this day we had light winds from the westward, and clear, pleasant weather. I got a passport from the Commissary of Marine, and am now only waiting for a passage to St. Gilles.

March 26th. Light winds from the southward with rain during the whole day, still waiting an opportunity to leave the island for the continent.

March 27th. Throughout this day pleasant breezes from the N. N. E. and fine weather. At seven o'clock in the morning, I embarked on board the *chasse-marée Mariana,* Captain Brumel, and after a pleasant passage of three hours, arrived safe at St. Gilles—a small seaport town on the west coast of France, lying in lat. 46° 40' north, long. 1° 51' west. It is an inconsiderable place, and only navigable for small vessels.

At two o'clock in the afternoon, I left this place on horseback for Sables d'Olonne, at which place I arrived at six o'clock in the evening and put up for the night. This is a pleasant little sea-port town, about five leagues from St. Gilles.

March 28th. Fresh breezes from the S. E. and cloudy weather throughout this day. At ten o'clock this morning, left this place with the courier for Napoleon, where I arrived at three o'clock in the afternoon, having travelled seven leagues in a miserable vehicle.

Napoleon is a newly built town, with several fine houses and broad streets. I had now got into the great public road, and after agreeing to pay sixty *francs* for my passage to La Rochelle, left Napoleon in the same vehicle at five o'clock in the afternoon. At eight o'clock in the evening, we arrived at the small village of Maria, and after having travelled about five leagues, we put up here for the night.

March 29th. We left Maria at five o'clock in the morning, and travelled on the great public road. We passed through Lucan and several other towns and villages, and arrived at La Rochelle (eighteen leagues from Napoleon), at five o'clock in the afternoon of the same day.

Here I put up at the Hôtel des Ambassadeurs, where I was delighted to meet with many of my countrymen, and once more to hear the sweet sound of my native language. I found lying here four American vessels, the privateer brig *Rattlesnake,* Captain Moffatt, of Philadelphia; letter-of-marque brig *Ida,* Captain Jeremiah Mantor, of Boston; letter-of-marque schooner *Commodore Decatur,* Captain Brown, of Philadelphia, and also a merchant brig, Captain Smith. Besides the captains of these vessels, there were here several American gentlemen, supercargoes, waiting for passages to return to the United States. For several days after my arrival at La Rochelle, we were without news from Paris, as all communication had been cut off, and not a diligence was allowed to run on the road between the two cities. The town was placed in a very anxious state of suspense; everybody knew that the allied armies were in the neighbourhood of Paris, and no one dared to speak a syllable on the subject At this time the military officers were seen conversing with each other in little groups, and appeared to be the only men that the government could rely upon.

At length, on the 2nd of April, 1814, news arrived in town that Paris had been taken by the allied armies on the 30th *ultimo.* The next day official orders arrived from Paris proclaiming the change of government. In the capitulation Bonaparte was sent to Elba, and Louis XVIII. was acknowledged King of France.

In a few minutes someone mounted a white cockade, and very soon after it became general, and now it was, "*Vive le Roi*," "*Vive Louis XVIII*."

Although at that time I was no friend of the Emperor, I was absolutely disgusted with several poor devils who a few days before this great event had extolled "*Le grand Empereur*" up to the skies, and now turned against him and called him "*le prince des tyrans*." This implication does not apply at all to the military, nor to the respectable part of the inhabitants, but to some hotel keepers and other mean-spirited turncoats, such as infest every part of the globe.

The *Rattlesnake* had been lying here some weeks. She put in here after a successful cruise off the coast of Norway, and round the north coast of England. Captain Moffatt had taken a great many prizes on his last cruise: some he had manned and sent into port, others he had destroyed, and thus by his gallant conduct had rendered his country essential service in distressing the enemy. The *Rattlesnake* was a fine brig. I think she mounted fourteen guns, and was well officered and equipped. Captain Moffatt told me that he captured a British transport ship with troops, after a smart engagement, and that he had not a man killed in the action, and but one wounded; that person was his marine officer, a young man belonging to New York, who was wounded in one of his legs, and was here taken to the Hospital. He had the best medical aid, and was tenderly nursed by the Sisters of Charity. He was advised by surgical men to have his leg amputated, and was warned of the danger of delay.

He would not consent to the operation, giving for reason that it would spoil his dancing. The good Sisters, seeing the young man daily becoming weaker and weaker, were extremely anxious that he should become a Christian (meaning a Catholic). To gratify them he consented (at least in appearance); they were rejoiced, thinking no doubt, they had been the means of saving the soul of a heretic. The poor fellow lingered a few weeks, and was followed to the grave by all the Americans in this place.

The *chasse-marée* that I chartered in Bordeaux to bring to this place hundred casks of wine and fifty pipes of brandy, I found lying here waiting orders with respect to its disposition. Captain Mantor, who was bound to Boston in ballast, offered to take the wine and brandy at a very low freight, *viz.* at $45 per ton.

The *Ida* was a fine coppered brig of 272 tons burden, mounting eight long nine and twelve pounders, with a complement of thirty-five men. The cost of the wine and brandy, including the freight and charges bringing it round to this port, amounted to twenty-five thousand *francs*, or say about five thousand dollars. We soon struck a bargain, and the next day put it on board his vessel, which, on the morning of the 8th of April, 1814, sailed from this port in company with the brig *Rattlesnake,* Captain Moffatt, of Philadelphia, and the letter-of-marque schooner *Commodore Decatur,* Captain Brown, also of Philadelphia.

These three vessels ran down on the north side of L'Isle de Ré, namely between the island and the main-land. In this passage they met an English man-of-war brig and a schooner in company, and were all driven back.

The *Rattlesnake* and the *Commodore Decatur* returned into port again. The *Ida* lay to off the east end of the island long enough to discharge his pilot, and then made a bold dash down the south side of the island, in plain sight of the British fleet that was lying at anchor in the roads off La Rochelle. I will here digress from the thread of my narrative, to insert the two following letters; as they have an intimate connection with this subject, I think it is better to place, them here, than to leave them to a later date.

Captain Jeremiah Mantor, formerly of the brig *Ida* of Boston;

Dear Sir :—Upon the score of old acquaintance, I herewith take the liberty of writing to you on the subject of the scenes through which we passed in our late war with England, in the years 1813 and 1814. I have been for several months writing a narrative of all the voyages I ever made, namely, from the year 1798, until I retired from the sea, in 1841.

Now, my dear sir, you doubtless recollect that I commanded the letter-of-marque schooner *David Porter,* of New
York, and that after I sent my vessel home from off L'Isle
Dieu, coast of France, I went on to La Rochelle, where we
met on the 29th of March, 1814; and you will also recollect that,I shipped by you in the brig *Ida,* hundred casks
of wine and fifty pipes of brandy for Boston. I had no
insurance on this property, and was of course extremely
anxious for your safety. I recollect that you sailed from
La Rochelle on the morning of the 8th of April, in company with the privateer brig *Rattlesnake,* Captain Moffatt,
of Philadelphia, and the letter-of-marque schooner *Commodore Decatur,* Captain Brown, also of Philadelphia, and
that you all three ran down between L'Isle de Ré and
the main-land, and in that passage you met an English
man-of-war brig with a schooner in company, sent there
to guard and block up the passage, and that you were all
driven back.

The *Rattlesnake* and *Commodore Decatur* returned into port
again, and off the east end of L'Isle de Ré you squared
away and dashed down the south side of the island, and
had to pass through the British fleet. At that time there lay
at anchor in the roads off La Rochelle, the *Queen Charlotte,* and four ships of the line. I understood that one of
these line-of-battle ships slipped her cables and made sail
in pursuit of your brig. Although I was at the time of your
sailing standing on the quay at La Rochelle, I still have but
an imperfect idea of all that passed. And now, my dear sir,
you would do me a great favour by giving me a detailed
account of all you can recollect of your marvellous escape;
namely, the length of your passage home, the number of
shot fired at you during the chase, and whether they threw
more than one shot on board of your brig, and any other
incidents you can call to mind will be gratefully received.
Your bravery and good conduct in evading the close pursuit of so many ships of war, ought to be published to

the world. You certainly out-manoeuvred and out-sailed them all, and I am satisfied that your prompt decision and gallant conduct saved the whole of the property entrusted to you.

For this and many other kind favours, I remain your obliged and very grateful friend,

George Coggeshall.

New York, January 5th, 1846.

West Tisbury, Mass.,
Martha's Vineyard, Jan. 17th, 1846.

Captain George Coggeshall:

Dear Sir:—I received your letter of the 5th inst., and am happy to hear from one of my old acquaintances. I often think of them and the scenes I have passed through during the years I have spent on the ocean. The voyage you speak of is well remembered, and it would not be possible, after the lapse of so many years, for me to give you a correct account of all my voyages during the late war, but I will write you the particulars of that passage home, and you can make what use of it you think proper.

I left La Rochelle in company with the *Rattlesnake* and *Commodore Decatur,* and run out north of L'Isle de Ré, with a fair wind. Saw two men-of-war ahead, hauled our wind and stood back to the east end of L'Isle de Ré. I saw there was a risk in returning again into port, and might be taken there, so I determined at once to make a bold push, discharged my pilot, and made all sail to pass the south end of the island. I saw in a moment several of the men-of-war under way upon my lee quarter. I was looking out for ships ahead, and as I opened the island, a schooner came down on my starboard side within musket shot; she gave me a broadside and three cheers, shot away my studding-sail boom and main-stay, and some small rigging. I soon passed her, but the men-of-war were coming up under my lee, and the shot flying thick.

I soon saw another ship bearing down upon my starboard

side. There was but one way to escape, which was, up helm and bring all astern, or sink; this was quickly done, and we crossed the bows of the head ship so near that I could hear them halloo on board plainly.

The shot went most of it over me: one thirty-two pounder raked my deck and lodged in the bows, one cut my anchor off the bows and cut the chains at the same moment. I cut the cable and let the anchor go. My crew were on the other side of the deck, and in the hold heaving out ballast, which saved many lives.

The vessels continued the chase until eleven at night, after that I saw no more of them. I think there were as many as eight or ten in pursuit of me. I stood out to sea, and at daylight saw two frigates right ahead, and had just time to haul upon the wind, not knowing but that I should upset, as I had lightened the brig so much that night; I had thrown overboard six nine-pounders during the night, and soon found her ready for another chase.

At dark I had gained four or five miles upon them; one was on my lee quarter, and the other astern. I was headed into the bay, and dare not risk to get before the wind.

About 9 p. m. the shutter to the binnacle fell, and they saw my light. They made signals one to the other, and that showed me where they were. I immediately bore up before the wind, and at daylight saw them hull down. I now had once more the wide ocean, but my brig was light, which made my passage rather long. I think it was twenty-six days.

Nothing more worth relating took place during our passage. I made two voyages to France, and one to New Orleans in the war, and passed through many scenes which often come to my mind, now I have set down in my old age to think of the many dangers and escapes that I have passed through.

I shall be happy to hear from you at any time.

Yours with respect, Jeremiah Mantor.

I will now continue my narrative, and return to the 9th of April, 1814. After the *Ida* had made her escape, and the *Rattlesnake* and *Commodore Decatur* returned into port, these two vessels were watched and blockaded with more vigilance than ever. The English men-of-war anchored nearer the port, while a brig and a schooner were almost constantly within gunshot of the harbour. Tranquillity having been restored in Paris, all the wheels of government began to move in a more regular train; the mails and diligences commenced running throughout the kingdom as formerly.

In a few days I settled all my business, and left this place in the diligence for Bordeaux, on the 12th of April, 1814, passing through Rochefort and several other towns lying on the great public road, and on the 14th, namely, two days after leaving La Rochelle, I once more had the pleasure to return in safety to Bordeaux. Here I found everything tranquil, and although the city was in the hands of the English, there was no noise or confusion.

The theatres were all open as usual, and well supported. In lien of seeing French troops and sentinels about the town, there were English and Portuguese soldiers stationed at every military post.

I found my business had been well managed by my good friends Messrs. Brun *frères*; a portion of my freight had been collected, and everything was in a successful train. The English had thus far respected private persons and private property.

There were no American vessels here; nearly all of them had left this country. There were a few however in the northern ports, namely, three blockaded at La Rochelle as before stated. The letter-of-marque schooner *Kemp*, Captain Jacobs, of Baltimore, was lying at Nantes, and the schooners *Lion* and *Spencer* at L'Orient. These were about all the American vessels left in the western ports of France. There were several American gentlemen, supercargoes, at Bordeaux and La Rochelle, waiting an opportunity to return home to the United States. Nearly all the American captains and supercargoes at this time in France were well known to each other, and were upon very friendly terms. I found here, as in all parts of the world, that mutual interest and mutual sympathy draw men closely together. We were all devising means to get home, some going to Amelia Island in neutral vessels, others taking passage in letters-of-marque, and some few in ships of war.

A few days before I arrived at Bordeaux, on the 10th of April, there was a terrible battle fought between the French and English armies at Toulouse. The French army was commanded by Marshal Soult, and the English by Lord Wellington. This was a most sanguinary conflict. Although the English were victorious, they lost, in killed and wounded, about five thousand men, and the French about three thousand. I saw great numbers of English officers who were brought down to Bordeaux sadly maimed, some with the loss of their limbs, others cut and mutilated in a frightful manner. These sights and scenes were absolutely enough to sicken one with war.

I had now so far arranged all my commercial affairs in Bordeaux, with my friends Messrs. Brun *frères*, that I thought seriously of returning to the United States, by the first good opportunity. Thus, after staying in this city six days, I left it again on the 21st of April, to return to La Rochelle in search of a passage home. I took the diligence and travelled on the great public road along the sea-coast, and arrived in two days at La Rochelle. Here I found the *Rattlesnake* and *Commodore Decatur* still blockaded, and as it appeared altogether uncertain when they would be able to get to sea, after remaining here about a fortnight, I concluded to proceed to Nantes.

I accordingly left La Rochelle on the 10th of May; travelled on the grand route, and passing through Morcilles, Napoleon, and several towns and villages, arrived at Nantes on the 11th of May. The distance from La Rochelle to this place is 100 miles. I stopped at the Hotel de France for a few days, and then took private lodgings with Captain Jacobs, of the letter-of-marque schooner *Kemp*, of Baltimore. This schooner was anchored at Paimbœuf, near the mouth of the river Loire, about thirty miles below Nantes. I made frequent excursions with Captain Jacobs down to Paimbœuf, and found the river very shallow and full of flats and sand bars, and very difficult to ascend except for small vessels. There is, however, water enough at the port of Paimbœuf, and the anchorage is good and safe. The shores and meadows along the river in the summer season are beautiful. The grounds are highly cultivated, and the houses and cottages are neat and pretty. Nantes is a fine old city, lying in lat. 47° 13' N., long. 1° 33 W., about 210 miles in a direct line S.W. of Paris. By Orleans, Blois, Tours, and other towns on the Loire, the distance is about 300 miles. It is generally well built, and has a great many public squares. The quays along the river are very fine, and shaded by rows of large elm trees, which render them delightful promenades.

Nantes was formerly one of the largest, if not the largest, commercial town in France, and is still a place of considerable importance in a commercial point of view. It numbers from one hundred and eighty to two hundred thousand inhabitants, and is, in my opinion, the most moral town of its size in the kingdom. Provisions are cheap, and taking everything into consideration, it is a very desirable residence, and strangers in pursuit of health and reasonable living, will find themselves quiet and comfortable in this highly favoured place. At the time I visited this town, there appeared to be about three women to one man, the male population having been taken away in great numbers for the last twenty years, to fill up the armies of France, which of course left a very large proportion of females.

I have before said I came on here for the purpose of obtaining a passage to the United States; but in this I was disappointed; there were no other American vessels here but the *Kemp*, and she was preparing to return home as a cruising vessel—that is to say, to pick up a cargo from the enemy on the ocean, if possible, and perhaps man and send into port a fast sailing rich prize or two, if fortunate enough to meet with such. This mode of cruising, though pleasant enough as a captain, did not meet my views as a passenger or a volunteer. I therefore concluded to return to Bordeaux again, and wait a more favourable opportunity to return home. I found Captain Jacobs a pleasant, gentlemanly man, and parted with him with sincere regret. After spending about a month of perfect leisure at Nantes, I left this agreeable place in the diligence for Bordeaux, on the 13th of June, 1814. The distance between the two cities is 216 miles, and the fare, including the expenses on the way, was 97 *francs*. We were two days on the road, and arrived in Bordeaux on the 15th, without accident; and I now had abundance of leisure, not only to look after my commercial affairs in Bordeaux, but to partake of its various amusements, and enjoy its hospitable society.

On the 9th of August I received the account sales of my cottons, with a statement of what was due me, and also the balance due for freight, all of which was now settled to my entire satisfaction. I forthwith remitted to my owners in New York, in sundry bills of exchange, $8,692, besides leaving a large balance in the hands of my worthy friends, Messrs. Brun *frères*; and thus, I am happy to say, I surmounted one difficulty after another, until things began to wear a brighter aspect; and as I was unable to obtain a passage from any of the ports on the western coast, I decided to go up to Paris and spend a few weeks, and try to get a passage home from some of the northern ports of France.

Before leaving this place, it would be ungrateful in me not to speak of the kind hospitality I received in this town; even amidst war and confusion, the rites of hospitality are here never forgotten. The kind treatment to strangers by the inhabitants of Bordeaux is proverbial, and needs no repetition from me. Still, I am happy to bear my feeble testimony, and time will never efface from my memory the happy days I have spent in this delightful city.

On the 15th of August, I left Bordeaux in the diligence for the capital. We passed through Angoulême, Poictiers, Tours, and along the pleasant banks of the Loire to Blois, Orleans, and from thence to Paris. The time occupied in performing this journey was five days, and the distance 130 post leagues, and the whole expense, including the fee to the conductor, postillion, servants,

&c., &c., was 196 *francs*. I put up at the Hôtel Strasbourg, in the Rue Notre Dame des Victoires. We got into the vicinity of this magnificent city just before the dawn of day. A young American friend was my travelling companion, and we were at daylight on the *qui vive* to catch the first glimpse of this vast metropolis, when just as the sun was rising we ascended a hill, and behold! the famed city of Paris was in full view. Among the many objects of admiration that caught the eye, the dome of the Hôtel des Invalides was the most conspicuous; it was newly gilded, and when the sun shone upon this splendid object, the effect was truly enchanting. I was young and enthusiastic at that time, and shall never forget the impression made on my mind by this, my first view of this astonishing city.

It was absolutely like transporting one to another world. I had read its history from my boyish days, and now, for the first time, beheld it in all its magnificence and sublimity. Since that time I have visited many parts of the globe, and even down to this date, 1846, I have never met its equal. London, certainly, covers a greater space, and has almost double the number of inhabitants; still, there never was, nor ever will be, but one Paris.

Immediately on my arrival in Paris, I wrote the following letter to the several owners of the *David Porter*:

Paris, 20th August, 1814.

Messrs. Lawrence & Whitney, James Lovett, Esq., and the other owners of the *David Porter*:

Gentlemen:—I have this moment arrived here from Bordeaux. I came here in hopes of obtaining a passage home in the ship *John Adams*, from Amsterdam, which ship, I am informed, is to sail in about a week from this day for America. I need not tell you my disappointment to learn from several American gentlemen who are here, that they, with several others in London, have applied to our Minister for a passage in said ship, and have been refused, and that it is absolutely impossible to obtain a passage in the *John Adams* on any terms.

How, or in what way, I shall get home, I am not able to

say, but assure you I shall embrace the first opportunity. It was not until the 9th instant, that I got my business settled with Brun *frères*. Enclosed I send you one set of bills of exchange, amounting together to $8,691, all of which, I trust, will be paid, without any difficulty; if they are not, the persons from whom I bought them are fully able to pay them, should they be returned. I enclose you, also, account sales of our cotton. Independent of what I now remit you, I have left in the hands of Messrs. Brun *frères* about 40,000 *francs*. What I now remit you, with what I have left in the hands of Brun *frères*, all belong to the joint concern of the owners of the *David Porter*, when the voyage is settled, except a small sum due to my officers.

The amount of Messrs. Archibald Gracie & Sons' cotton, I have remitted to them in a bill of exchange on a gentleman in Baltimore. At present, the exchange between this country and England is 23½ *francs* per pound sterling, which is nearly at par, consequently unfavourable to remit to the United States by way of England; and as I am unable to obtain any more good bills on the United States, I rather think I shall leave the remainder of the funds with Brun *frères*, where they will be safe, at the same time gaining four *per cent* interest *per annum*. The enclosed bills I bought at from nine to ten *per cent*. below par.

As you may suppose, I am very much fatigued after so long a journey; but for fear my letter will not be in time to go by the *John Adams*, I am obliged to write this in haste, which I hope you will receive as an apology for my not writing more particularly.

I hope before long I shall be able to find a passage home some way or other, when I trust I shall have the pleasure to explain everything to your satisfaction.

As I am too late to write any of my friends by this opportunity, please advise them the substance of this letter, and oblige

Your obedient servant,   George Coggeshall.

After having delivered several letters of introduction from my friend in Bordeaux, I occupied myself for some days attending to commercial business, and among other things, purchased five thousand *francs* worth of French silks, shawls, silk stockings, &c. These articles were all carefully packed and dispatched to Bordeaux, to be shipped by the first fast sailing American schooner that should leave that place for the United States. When this was accomplished, I commenced visiting the various museums, libraries, public gardens, palaces, &c. It being a fine season of the year, I also made excursions to St. Cloud, Versailles, St. Germain, St. Denis, and other places in the neighbourhood of the metropolis.

There are in this great city so many objects of curiosity, that a stranger may spend several months with pleasure and profit in visiting them.

The day before I left Paris, I wrote the following letter:—

Paris, September, 8th, 1814.

Messrs. Archibald Gracie & Sons:

Gentlemen:—I send you enclosed a bill of exchange for $991, on James Williams, Esq., of Baltimore. This is the net proceeds of your fifty-one bales of cotton. By the ship *John Adams*, I forwarded you one set of these bills and account sales. I also sent one copy to L'Orient, to be forwarded. This, I shall send to England, to go by the *Cartel*, which, I am told, is now fitting for the U. S.

I am extremely sorry, gentlemen, your shipment of cotton has turned out so much to your disadvantage. I however hope you will do me the justice to believe I have done the best I could in the business. I came on here for the purpose of getting a passage in the *John Adams* from Amsterdam, but was disappointed, as they are not allowed to take passengers. I am also informed that the *Cartel*, which is now fitting away from England, takes none but prisoners. I shall, therefore, leave here tomorrow morning for Bordeaux, and endeavour to get a passage to Amelia Island, or the West Indies, and from thence home, when I hope I shall have the pleasure to explain everything relating to your shipment to your satisfaction.

I am, gentlemen, with respect and regard,

Your obedient servant,

George Coggeshall.

P. S. I wrote by the schooner *Commodore Decatur,* brig *Rattlesnake,* and *Commodore Perry,* which letters I fear you have never received, as it is here reported that all those vessels have been captured.

Yours truly,

G. C.

At this period there was but a small number of American gentlemen in Paris, consequently they were generally known to each other.

The Ambassador from the United States, residing here, was the Hon. Wm. H. Crawford. He was highly respected and esteemed by the Americans, and seemed to take pleasure in acts of kindness and benevolence to his countrymen. From a turbulent state of war and confusion, Paris had lately become quiet and tranquil. Louis XVIII., and other members of the royal family, used almost daily to show themselves from the balcony of the Tuileries, and I frequently saw the Duke and Duchess of Angoulême riding on horseback in various parts of the city.

The theatres and all public places of amusement were open, and appeared to be well patronized and supported. There were vast numbers of strangers here from different parts of Europe, and everybody seemed to be in pursuit of pleasure.

After having spent twenty days amidst these gay scenes, I left Paris on the 9th of September, 1814, in the diligence, and returned by the same route by which I came up, passing through Orleans and down along the banks of the Loire, and so on to Bordeaux, where I arrived on the 13th of September, without accident.

I had many kind friends in this city, and returned to it with pleasure, but found those from America were daily diminishing; some returning home in neutral ships, by way of the West Indies and Amelia Island; others going to Holland to take passage from that country. My friend Robert R. Stewart, Esq., of Philadelphia, after waiting several months for a passage to the United States, had left this place for L'Orient, in hopes of getting a passage from that city to the United States with Captain Blakely, in the *Wasp*. This ship, after having captured the British sloop-of-war *Reindeer*, put into L'Orient for supplies, and here Mr. Stewart joined her. They sailed from that place on the 27th of August, 1814, bound on a cruise for several months, and at the expiration of the appointed time intended to return to the United States.

A few days after leaving port she made several prizes, and on the evening of the 1st of September, she engaged and captured the British sloop-of-war *Avon,* of 18 guns. A few minutes after this ship had surrendered, the English brig-of-war *Castilian,* of 18 guns, fired one broadside into the *Wasp,* and then hauled off and escaped in the darkness of the night. There is scarcely a doubt that the *Wasp* would have taken the *Castilian* also, if they had been favoured with daylight. While on board the *Wasp,* Mr. Stewart joined the marine corps, as a volunteer, and thus assisted under the brave Blakely to vanquish the enemies of his country.

About the middle of September, the *Wasp* took and destroyed two British brigs; and on the 21st of the same month, in lat. 33° 12' north, long. 14° 56' west, she captured the British armed brig *Atalanta*. This being a valuable prize, Captain Blakely determined to send her into port. He put on board of her as prize-master, Midshipman Geisinger, and a prize crew. In this brig, Mr. Stewart went as passenger. She arrived safely at Savannah on the 14th of November, 1814. These two gentlemen and the prize crew are all that escaped from the ever-to-be-lamented *Wasp* and her gallant crew. I take pleasure in stating these facts, that the patriotic conduct of my friend may be known to the world, as I have never seen his name mentioned in connection with the ill-fated *Wasp* (in any official account), and I deem it but a matter of common justice to record my knowledge of these facts. There were very many patriotic individuals during our late war with England who rendered essential service to their country and are entitled to its gratitude, whose acts, I am sorry to say, are almost entirely unknown; for instance, my worthy friends Mantor, of the *Ida,* and Stewart, who was a volunteer on board the victorious *Wasp.*

While in Bordeaux, I heard the gratifying news of the safe arrival of the schooner *David Porter,* at Gloucester, Cape Ann, and also of the arrival of the brig *Ida,* at Boston. After I left the *David Porter,* at L'Isle Dieu, under the command of Mr. Nichols, he captured on his passage home several British prizes, from which vessels he loaded the schooner, and carried with him into port ten prisoners. Soon after his arrival at Cape Ann, he proceeded with the *David Porter* to Boston, at which place the vessel and cargo were consigned to the respectable house of Messrs. Munson & Barnard, at that place. These gentlemen sold both vessel and cargo at high prices. They also sold the brandy and wine, by the brig *Ida,* at a very good profit, and closed the whole concern to the entire satisfaction of all parties. I think the schooner sold for $10,000, and was soon fitted out as a regular privateer, and I believe was afterwards very successful.

Messrs. Munson &. Barnard also received from the government of the United States, $1,000 as a bounty on the ten prisoners.

The trunk of goods which I purchased in Paris for 5,000 *francs*, or say $1,000, was shipped by my friends in Bordeaux, on board the Baltimore schooner *Transit,* Captain Richardson. This vessel arrived in New York on or about the 8th of March 1815, and this trunk of goods sold at auction for $2,075.

Bordeaux, Oct. 1st., 1814.

I had now closed the voyage of the *David Porter,* so far as it devolved upon me, and will here close the subject with a few remarks.

When it is considered how many obstacles we met with, from the commencement of the voyage on the 14th day of Nov., 1813, until its conclusion, I think it will be conceded that we triumphed over many difficulties, and ultimately made a good voyage; and I am happy to add to the entire satisfaction of all the owners of the fortunate little schooner.

I will here insert the following letter to my brother Charles Coggeshall, second lieutenant of the letter-of-marque *David Porter,* at Milford, Connecticut.

Bordeaux, Oct. 21st, 1814.

Dear Charles:—I am now on the eve of leaving this place for L'Orient, to take command of the elegant American schooner *Leo.* I have been waiting several months to obtain a passage home to the United States, and have consented to take charge of this schooner, to proceed from France to Charleston or some other southern port.

Your cotton netted 903 *francs.* The account sales I have sent to Messrs. Lawrence and Whitney, and desired them to pay you the amount, together with the gain on the exchange, which is about ten *per cent.*

You may, perhaps, ask why I did not invest the amount in French goods, that you might have gained a larger profit. I answer that I did not feel myself authorized to hazard your property without your consent, the risk of capture being in my opinion very great.

I was very happy to hear of your safe arrival in the *David Porter.* Both Captain Nichols and yourself, and in fact, all the officers and men deserve a great deal of praise, and I do assure you I shall never forget your faithful and very friendly conduct during the whole voyage. Yes, Charles, although I sometimes scold a little when we are together, I need not tell you how dear you are to me and that your faithful and brave conduct has entirely won my heart. I hope you will study navigation, and improve your mind by reading while you remain at home, and thus qualify yourself to command a ship when the war is ended. Should the enemy dare to molest the part of the country where you may be, I hope and trust you will be among the first to drive them into the sea. Our father fought them in 1775, before he was as old as you are, and I hope he has not left a son who would not defend his country, if necessary, with his heart's blood.

We hear nothing from America but degrading defeats and losses of every kind. Washington burnt, beaten here and there, and everything appears to be going to the devil. If things go on no better, I shall be ashamed to acknowledge myself an American.

I shall write to mother and sister by the same vessel that conveys this to you.

Remember me affectionately to our brothers James and Francis, and believe me, my dear Charles,

Your sincere friend and brother,

George Coggeshall.

CHAPTER 4

Cruise and capture of the Letter-of-Marque Schooner *Leo*

The *Leo* was a fine Baltimore built vessel of 320 tons, a remarkably fast sailer, and in every respect a superior vessel. She was lying in the harbour of L'Orient on the 1st of November, 1814, and was then owned by Thomas Lewis, Esq., an American gentleman residing in Bordeaux. On the 2nd of November, she was purchased by an association of American gentlemen (then in France), placed under my command, and her commission as a letter-of-marque endorsed over to me under the sanction of Hon. William H. Crawford, who was at the time our minister at Paris. It was determined that I should make a short cruise for the purpose of capturing a few prizes from the enemy, and then proceed to Charleston for a cargo of cotton, and return as soon as possible to France.

As there were at the time quite a number of American seamen in Bordeaux, Nantes, and L'Orient, supported by the government of the United States through the consuls at those ports, it was desirable to take home as many of them as the schooner could conveniently accommodate.

I took with me as first officer, Mr. Pierre G. Depeyster, and left Bordeaux by diligence for L'Orient. On our way we stopped a day or two at Nantes, where I engaged, with the sanction of our consul at that port, forty seamen and two petty officers.

Mr. Azor O. Lewis, a fine young man, brother of the former

owner of the *Leo,* was one of my prize masters, and to him I committed the charge of bringing about forty more seamen from Bordeaux to L'Orient. The residue of the officers and men were picked up at L'Orient, with the exception of four or five of my petty officers, who came up from Bordeaux to L'Orient.

Early in November we commenced fitting the schooner for sea. We found her hull in pretty good order, but her sails and rigging were in a bad state. I, however, set everything in motion, as actively as possible, and put in requisition sail-makers, block-makers, blacksmiths, &c. &c, while others were employed taking in ballast, filling water casks, &c, in fine, hurrying on as fast possible, before we should be stopped.

The English had so much influence with the new government of Louis XVIII. that I felt extremely anxious to get out on the broad ocean without delay, and therefore drove on my preparations almost night and day.

After ballasting, I took on board three tons of bread, thirty barrels of beef, fifteen *ditto* of pork, and other stores to correspond, being enough for fifty days.

I got ready for sea on the 6th of November. My crew, including the officers and marines, numbered about one hundred souls, and a better set of officers and men never left the port of L'Orient. But we were miserably armed; we had, when I first took the command of the schooner, one long brass 12-pounder, and four small 4-pounders, with some fifty or sixty poor muskets. Those concerned in the vessel seemed to think we ought, with so many men, to capture prizes enough, even without guns. With this miserable armament I was now ready for sea, and only waiting for my papers from Paris. I was ordered by the public authorities to return into port and disarm the vessel. I was compelled to obey the order, and accordingly waited on the commanding officer, and told him it was a hard case, that I should not be allowed arms enough to defend the vessel against boats. He politely told me he was sorry, but that he must obey the orders of the government, and that I must take out all the guns except one, and at the same time laughingly observed that one gun was enough to take a dozen English ships before I got to Charleston.

I of course kept the long 12-pounder, and in the night smuggled on board some twenty or thirty muskets. In this situation I left the port of L'Orient, on the 8th of November, 1814, and stood out to sea in the hope of capturing a few prizes. After getting to sea we rubbed up the muskets, and with this feeble armament steered for the chops of the British Channel. I soon found that when the weather was good and the sea smooth, I could take merchantmen enough by boarding; but in rough weather the travelling 12-pounder was but a poor reliance, and not to be depended upon like the long centre gun that I had on board the *David Porter.*

It is true my officers and men were always ready to board an enemy of three times our force; but, in a high sea, if one of these delicately Baltimore-built vessels should come in contact with a large strong ship, the schooner would inevitably be crushed and sunk. For this reason, I was compelled to let one large English ship with twelve guns escape while in the English Channel, because the weather was too rough to board her.

On the 9th, boarded the French ship *Le Tartare,* sixty-eight days from St. Domingo, bound to Nantes, also a Dutch galliot from Ostend, bound to La Rochelle: Lat. by obs. 46° 17' North; Long. 4° 2' West.

Nov. 10th.—First part of this day moderate breezes, with cloudy weather and rain. During the remainder of the day we had strong gales from the N. N. W., with a high sea running. Lat. 46° 9' North.

Nov. 11th.—The day commenced with moderate breezes from the N. E. and pleasant weather. At 6 o'clock a. m. saw a sail bearing W. N. W., made all sail in chase; at 8 o'clock spoke the chase; she proved to be a *galliot* four days from Oberson, with a cargo of salt, bound for Ostend. Lat. by obs. 47° 5' North; Long. 6° 18' West.

Nov. 12th.—In the morning, light breezes and cloudy-weather. At 5 o'clock in the afternoon we spoke the *galliot Topsher,* from Bayonne, bound to Antwerp with a cargo of brandy. The day ended with strong gales at N. N. W. and a high sea running. Lat. 48° 49' N.; Long. 7° 40' W.

Nov. 13th.—This day commenced with strong breezes and cloudy weather. Spoke a Danish *galliot* from Malaga, bound to Amsterdam, also the French ship *Stanislaus* from Havre bound to Martinque. At 6 in the afternoon sounded in sixty-five fathoms water, the Scilly Islands bearing N. W. fifteen leagues distant. Light winds and variable through the night. At 6 a. m. saw a brig to windward. At 7 *ditto* she set English colours; gave her a gun, when she struck her flag. She proved to be an English brig from Leghorn, bound up the Channel. It now commenced blowing a strong breeze from the N. W., and soon there was a high sea running. Saw a large ship steering up the Channel; left the prize, made sail in chase of her. At 10 a. m. she set English colours, and fired a gun. Had the weather been smooth, I think we could have carried her by boarding in fifteen minutes, or had I met her at sea, I would have followed her until the weather was better and the sea smooth: but being now in the English Channel with a high sea, it would have destroyed my schooner if she had come in contact with this wall-sided ship. She showed six long nines on each side. After exchanging a few shot, I hauled off, and then returned to our prize. Fresh gales and cloudy weather.

Nov. 14th.—These twenty-four hours commenced with fresh breezes and cloudy weather. At 2 p. m. the weather moderated, when I took out of the English prize brig the captain, mate and crew, and put on board of her a prize-master and seven men, with orders to proceed to a port in the United States. At 4 p. m. saw a sail to windward, when we made sail in chase. At 8 *ditto* it became dark and squally; lost sight of the chase. At 8 a. m. saw our prize ahead; we soon came up with her, when I supplied her with two casks of water and a quantity of bread, and left her to proceed on her course to the United States.

Nov. 15th.—These twenty-four hours commenced with

fresh gales from the westward, with a rough sea running. Middle and latter part of these twenty-four hours, the wind continued to blow strong from the westward with a high sea. As it was now the middle of November, and no prospect of much fine weather, and my schooner so badly armed, I concluded to leave this rough cruising ground and run to the southward, in hopes of finding better weather, where I could profit by a superior number of men in making prizes. Lat. 47° 28' North.

Nov. 16th.—These twenty-four hours commenced with fresh gales at S. W, with a high sea. At midnight the wind suddenly shifted to the N. W., and blew a strong gale from that quarter: double reefed the lower sails, and stood to the southward. At 7 a. m. it moderated; saw a sail to the eastward; made sail in chase; at 9 *ditto*, boarded the chase. She proved to be the Spanish brig *Diligent,* Captain Joseph Antonio de Bard, from Bilboa, bound to London. Put eight English prisoners on board of her, with a tolerable supply of provisions, when he proceeded on his course. At 10 a. m. saw two sail to the westward, and made sail in chase. Lat. by obs. 47° 10' N.; Long. 8° 0' W.

Nov. 17th.—These twenty-four hours commenced with brisk breezes from the N. N. W., and cloudy weather. At 3 p. m. boarded the Spanish brig *Alonzo.* She was from Tenerife, bound to London. On board of this vessel I put the captain, late master of our prize brig. At 4 *ditto* spoke a *galliot* under Hamburg colours, from Bilboa, bound to Bristol, England. Four sail in sight, light airs and fine weather. Made sail in chase of the nearest vessel at noon. The chase hove to and hoisted Spanish colours. When about to board this brig, we discovered an English man-of-war very near, in full chase of us.

Nov. 18th.—Light winds and fine weather; the man-of-war brig still in chase of us, about two miles distant. At 8 p. m. light breezes from the southward; passed near a brig standing to the eastward; had not time to board her, as the man-of-war was still in chase. At midnight the wind became fresh from the W. S. W., with dark, rainy weather. Took in all the light sails, and hauled close upon the wind to the W. N. W. At 7 a. m. saw a small sail on our weather-bow; made sail in chase. At 10 *ditto* came up with and captured the chase; found it was an English cutter, from Tenerife, bound to London, with a cargo of wine.

Nov. 19th.—These twenty-four hours commenced with strong gales from the northward, and a high surf running. At meridian took out of the prize twenty quarter casks of wine, together with her sails, cables, rigging, blocks, &c, and after removing the prisoners, scuttled her. At 1 p. m. she sank. Strong gales from the northward and rainy weather during the night. At 7 a. m. saw a sail to windward; tacked ship to get the weather-gage. At 11 *ditto* got her on our lee beam, when I made her out to be an English brig-of-war of sixteen guns. I commenced firing my long twelve. At noon, after receiving about thirty, or forty shot from the enemy, without any material damage, I hauled off. Some of his shot passed over us, some fell short; and only one of his shot hulled us: this shot passed through our bends amidships, and lodged in the hold. I could out-sail him with the greatest ease, and if I had had a long well-mounted centre gun, I could have annoyed him without receiving any injury by keeping just out of reach of his carronades. These twenty-four hours ended with fresh gales from the N. W. with a high sea running. Lat. 47° 56' N.; long. 11° 9' W.

Nov. 20th.—These twenty-four hours commenced with fresh gales and variable squally weather. Two sail in sight; made sail in chase. At half-past 4 p. m. spoke one of them, which was a Hamburg barque from St. Thomas, bound home. At 7 *ditto* boarded a Dutch brig, from Faro, bound to Rotterdam, with a cargo of fruit, and, of course, permitted him to proceed on his course. During the night we had a continuation of strong gales, and bad weather, with much sea. At 11 a. m. saw a sail to the westward; at meridian came up with and boarded her. She proved to be the Dutch brig *Hope,* from Naples, bound to Amsterdam, with a cargo of wine. Lat. by obs. 46° 36' N.; long. 12° 22' west.

Nov. 21st.—These twenty-four hours commenced with fresh

winds from the N. N. E., and squally weather. At meridian saw a sail bearing W. S. W.; made sail in chase. At 4 p. m., she being directly to leeward, I ran down to discover the character of the chase; I soon made her out to be a frigate. When within three miles' distance, I hoisted an English ensign. The frigate showed Portuguese colours, and resorted to every stratagem in his power to decoy us down within the range of his shot. Finding I could out-sail him with ease, I hauled down the English colours, set an American ensign, and hauled close upon the wind, and soon lost sight of him. During the night we had fresh gales at E. N. E., and squally weather. At 7 a. m. saw a small sail bearing S. S. W.; made sail in chase. I soon came up with and boarded an English schooner from Malaga, bound to Dublin, with a cargo of fruit. Took out the prisoners and a supply of fruit, and then manned her and gave orders to the prize master to make the best of his way to the United States. Lat. by account 45° 33' N.; long. 12° 0' W.

Nov. 22nd.—These twenty-four hours commenced with light airs and fine pleasant weather. At 3 p. m. came up with and boarded a Danish *galliot*; at 12 o'clock, midnight, put ten English prisoners on board of her. I supplied them with provisions, and a quarter cask of wine, and the *galliot* proceeded on her voyage. She was from Marseilles, bound to Hamburg, with a cargo of wine and oil. At 8 a. m. saw a sail bearing N. N. E.; made sail in chase, and at eleven boarded her. She proved to be a Swedish *barque* from St. Ubes, bound to Stockholm. The day ends with dark, rainy, and gloomy weather, with considerable sea. Lat. by account 45° 53' N.; long. 13° 0' W.

Nov. 23rd.—These twenty-four hours commenced with fresh gales from the southward, with dark, rainy weather. At 1 p. m. wore ship to the S. E. in chase of a brig; at three came up with and spoke her. She proved to be a Prussian, from Oporto, bound to Hamburg, with a cargo of wine and fruit. Middle part of the twenty-four hours, strong gales from the N. N. W. At noon discovered two frigates to leeward. They both made sail in chase of me. I plied to windward, tacking every hour, and beat them with great ease; but, as there were two of them, I was not quite at ease until I had got out of their neighbourhood. These twenty-four hours end with strong breezes from the N. W., with showers of rain. Lat. by obs. 45° 8' N.; long. 13° 6' W.

Nov. 24th.—These twenty-four hours commenced with fresh gales from the N. W., and squally with showers of rain and a high head-sea running; the two frigates still in chase of us. At 5 p. m. the weathermost frigate was about ten or twelve miles distant to leeward; finding I could beat them with so much ease, I reefed the sails, and plied to windward. Towards morning the wind moderated, and at daylight there was nothing in sight. Lat. by obs. 44° 34' N., long. 15° 8' W.

Nov. 25th.—These twenty-four hours commenced with moderate breezes from the westward, and fine weather. At 3 p. m. discovered a sail bearing about S. E.; made sail and bore away in chase. At half-past three, made her out to be a frigate, when I hauled upon the wind. At four *ditto* she fired a gun, and showed American colours. I set an American ensign for a few minutes, and then hauled it down and hoisted a large English ensign. He fired three or four shot, but finding they fell short, stopped firing and crowded all sail in chase of me. Night coming on I soon lost sight of him. During the night we had fresh breezes and cloudy weather. At daylight there was nothing in sight; took in sail; during the remainder of these twenty-four hours we had fresh gales from the westward, with dark, thick weather. Lat. by obs. 43° 2' N.

Nov. 26th.—These twenty-four hours commenced with strong gales from the W. N. W., and thick, squally weather. At 1 p. m. discovered a sail to the windward, bearing N. W., made sail in chase, tacking every hour. At 5 *ditto*, made him out to be a ship standing upon the wind to the N. E. At half-past 9 o'clock, after getting on his weather quarter, ran up alongside, hailed him, and ordered him to heave to, which order was immediately obeyed. I sent my boat on board, and found him to be an English ship, burthen about 200 tons, from Palermo, bound to London, with a cargo of brimstone, rags, mats, &c. He mounted six guns, with a crew of about twenty men. We kept company through the night. The latter part of these twenty-four hours, light winds and fine weather. Lat. by obs. 42° 31' N., long. 15° 46' W.

Nov. 27th.—Commenced with light breezes from the N. W., and fine, pleasant weather. In the forenoon of this day removed the prisoners from the ship and put on board a prize master and a crew of ten men. I also took out his guns, powder, shot, and some fruit, and then ordered her to proceed to the United States. At 2 p. m. made sail and steered to the S. W., and at 5 *ditto* lost sight of the prize. These twenty-four hours end with light winds from the W. N. W., and cloudy weather. Lat. by obs. 41° 3' N.; long. 15° 46' W.

Nov. 28th.—These twenty-four hours commenced with a continuation of the same wind and weather, nothing in sight. During the night we had light winds and cloudy weather, with a little rain.

At 8 a. m. boarded a Dutch *galliot*, four days from Lisbon, bound to Rotterdam with a cargo of salt. Put the captain of the prize ship, his mate, and three of his crew, on board this *galliot*, which then proceeded on his voyage.

At noon brought to and boarded the Swedish brig *Johanna*, fourteen days from Dublin, in ballast, bound to Alicant.

The weather being fine, we painted the schooner. Lat. by obs. 39° 56' N.; long. 15° 16' W.

Nov. 29th.—These twenty-four hours commenced with light winds from the N. E. and fine weather: at midnight hove to— light winds and smooth sea.

At half past 6 a. m. daylight, saw a small sail bearing S. E.; at seven spoke her; she was a small schooner, one day from Lisbon, bound to Oporto. At this time made the Burling Rocks, bearing S. S. E. five leagues distant; several small sail in sight. At meridian the Rock of Lisbon bore S. by E. seven leagues distant. Fresh breezes from the N. E. and fine weather. Lat. by obs. 39° 1' N.

Nov. 30th.—These twenty-four hours commenced with light winds from the northward, with light squalls of rain. At 6 p. m. wore ship and stood off shore, and at midnight hove to.

At 7 a. m. saw a sail to the eastward. Made sail and soon spoke the chase, which proved to be the French brig *Two-Brothers,* one day from Lisbon, bound to Morlaix. At meridian the Rock of Lisbon bore East twelve leagues distant. Moderate breezes and cloudy weather. Lat. by obs. 38° 33' N.

Dec. 1st.—These twenty-four hours commenced with fresh breezes at N. N. W., with open cloudy weather.

At 1 p. m. saw a ship on our weather quarter, coming up with us very fast. I made sail, steering to the westward, to get to windward of the ship, in order to ascertain her character. It was then blowing a strong breeze from the N. N. W., and the weather was somewhat squally; a head-sea was running. About half-past 2 p. m. the schooner gave a sudden pitch, when, to the astonishment of every person on board, the foremast broke, about one-third below its head, and in a moment after it broke again, close to the deck. While in this situation, I had the mortification to see the ship pass us, within pistol-shot, without being able to pursue her. I believe she was an English packet, which was just out of Lisbon, and bound for England; and, I doubt not, if this unfortunate accident had not occurred, we should have captured her in less than one hour from the time she was first seen. At this time the packets transported large quantities of specie to England, and this ship would, in all probability, have proved a rich prize to us. I have no doubt the mast was defective, and that it should have been renewed before leaving port. From this untoward circumstance, resulted all the misfortunes attending the cruise.

I cannot express the disappointment and mortification I now felt, not so much on my own account, as for the loss incurred by the gentlemen who planned and fitted out the expedition. The Rock of Lisbon bore E. S. E., eighty miles distant, and my only hope was to get into Lisbon or St. Ubes before daylight the next morning, and thus escape capture. I accordingly cleared away the wreck, rigged a jury foremast, and bore away. At 4 p. m., an hour after the accident occurred, we were going at the rate of seven knots an hour, and had the breeze continued through the night, should have got into port by daylight next morning. But, unfortunately, the wind became light during the night, and we made little progress. At 5 a. m., daylight, made Cape Espartel and the Rock of Lisbon, when it became almost calm. We then commenced sweeping and towing, with two boats ahead, until 1 p. m., when a light air sprung up from the westward, and I had strong hopes of being able to get in, or run the vessel on shore and destroy her, and thus escape capture.

At 2 p. m., being about four miles from the land, I received a Lisbon pilot on board. The ebb-tide now commenced running out of the Tagus, and I had the mortification to see a British frigate coming out with the first of it, with a light breeze from off the land. At 2 p. m. I was under her guns. She proved to be the *Granicus,* a thirty-eight gun frigate, Captain W. F. Wise. We were all removed to the frigate, and the schooner taken in tow for Gibraltar.

Two days after our capture, *viz.* on the 3rd of December, we arrived at Gibraltar. Nearly all my officers and my men were distributed and sent to England in different ships; the first and second lieutenants, with myself, were retained on board the *Granicus* to undergo an examination at the admiralty court.

The next day after our arrival the frigate left port for Tetuan Bay, Morocco, opposite Gibraltar, to obtain water and to be painted. We were taken on this little voyage, and had I not been a prisoner, I should have enjoyed very much the novelty of the excursion, which occupied three or four days. Captain Wise was a fine, gentlemanly man, and always treated me and my officers with respect and kindness. We messed in the ward-room, and I had a state-room to myself, and was as comfortable and happy as I could be under the circumstances.

I used to dine with Captain Wise almost daily; he frequently said to me, "Don't feel depressed by captivity, but strive to forget that you are a prisoner, and imagine that you are only a passenger."

He also invited my first lieutenant, Mr. Depeyster, occasionally to dine with him, and said he would endeavour to get us paroled, and thus prevent our being sent to England. We stated to him, that we had voluntarily released more than thirty British prisoners notwithstanding the American government gave a bounty (to letters-of-marque and privateers) of one hundred dollars per head for British prisoners brought into the United States. These facts, Captain Wise represented to the governor, and also added, that the five English prisoners, found on board the *Leo,* said they had been very kindly treated, and he hoped His Excellency would release me and my two lieutenants upon our parole, and let us return direct to the United States.

The governor refused to comply with the kind request of Captain Wise, and said he had positive orders from the British government to send every American prisoner, brought to that port, to England. When Captain Wise informed us that he was unable to obtain our liberty on parole, he gave me a letter of introduction to a friend in England, requesting him to use his best interest to get myself and my first and second lieutenants released on parole, and thus enable us to return forthwith to the United States. Mr. Daly, an Irish gentleman, second lieutenant of the *Granicus,* who was connected with several persons of distinction in England, also gave me a letter to a noble lady of great influence at court. I regret I do not recollect her name, but I well remember the emphatic expression of the kind-hearted and generous Daly when he handed me the letter to his noble friend.

"Cause this letter to be presented," said he, "and rely upon it this lady will never allow you or your two friends to be sent to prison in England." Mr. Depeyster was a high-spirited man, and when he learned that we could not obtain our liberty on parole, he became extremely vexed and excited, and told the ward-room officers that if it should ever please God to place him in a letter-of-marque or privateer, during the war, he would never again release an English prisoner, but would have a place built in the vessel to confine them until he should arrive in the

United States; that the bounty of one hundred dollars given by the United States government rendered it an object to carry them into port, but from motives of humanity we had released many of their countrymen; and now they refused to parole three unfortunate men who were in their power. I said but little on the subject, but from that moment resolved to make my escape upon the first opportunity.

The next day after this conversation (December 8th), Captain Wise said "Captain Coggeshall, it is necessary that you and your officers should go on shore to the admiralty office, there to be examined with respect to the condemnation of your schooner, your late cruise, &c, and if you will pledge me your word and honour that you and your officers will not attempt to make your escape, I will permit you and the other two gentlemen to go on shore without a guard."

I told him at once that I would give the pledge not to attempt in any way to make my escape, and would also be answerable for Mr. Depeyster and Mr. Allen. This ready compliance on my part resulted from a desire to gain an opportunity to reconnoitre the garrison, or in seamen's phrase, "to see how the land lay," in order to profit by the first chance to make my escape when not on parole.

We accordingly went on shore without a guard, and were conducted to the admiralty office. I was first examined, and was asked a great many questions, the greater part of which were from a printed copy: the answers were written down opposite the questions. It seemed to me to be more a matter of form, than for any special purpose. By the by, many of the inquiries appeared to me very unmeaning and unimportant. When they had finished with me, they commenced with Mr. Depeyster; and after asking him a few questions, the court of inquiry was adjourned until the next morning at 10 o'clock; and notifying us to be there precisely at the time appointed, we were dismissed. We then took a stroll about the town for an hour or two, returned on board, and reported ourselves to Captain Wise.

Thus far, not a shadow of suspicion had been visible on the

countenances of Captain Wise, or his officers, that either of us would attempt to make our escape. In the evening, I consulted with Messrs. Depeyster and Allen on the subject of giving them the dodge upon the very first opportunity. I told them that if the captain required my parole the next morning I would not give it, neither would I advise them to pledge their word and honour that they would not make their escape. I told them, furthermore, that I was resolved to slip away the first moment I saw a favourable opportunity, and would advise them to do the like, and not, from any motives of delicacy, to wait a moment for me.

The next morning, when dressing, I put all the money I had, say about one hundred twenty-*franc* gold pieces, in a belt that was around my person, and some fifteen or twenty Spanish dollars in my pocket, with some little relics and trifling keepsakes. Thus prepared, I went to breakfast in the wardroom. About 9 o'clock Captain Wise sent for me, when the following dialogue ensued:

"Well, Coggeshall, I understand you and your officers are required at the admiralty office at 10 o'clock, and if you will again pledge your honour, as you did yesterday, that you will neither of you attempt to make your escape, you may go on shore without a guard, otherwise I shall be obliged to send one with you."

I watched his countenance closely, for a moment, to ascertain his real meaning, and whether he was determined to adhere strictly to the words he had just uttered, and then replied, "Captain Wise, I am surprised that you should think it possible for anyone to make his escape from Gibraltar."

He instantly saw I was sounding him, when he pleasantly but firmly said, "Come, come, it won't do, you must either pledge your word and honour that neither you nor your officers will attempt to make your escape, or I shall be compelled to send a guard with you."

I felt a little touched, and promptly replied, "You had better send a guard, sir."

Accordingly, he ordered the third lieutenant to take a sergeant and four marines with him and conduct us to the admiralty office.

At the hour appointed they recommenced the examination where they had left off the day before with Mr. Depeyster. I was sitting in the court-room, and Mr. Allen standing at the door, when he beckoned to me. I instantly went to the door, and found the lieutenant had left his post, and was not in sight. I then asked the sergeant whether he would go with us a short distance up the street to take a glass of wine. He readily complied with my request, leaving the marines at the door to watch Mr. Depeyster, and walked respectfully at a few paces behind us, up the street. (I had been once before at Gibraltar, and understood the town perfectly well.)

We soon came to a wine shop on a corner with a door opening on each street. While the soldier was standing at the door, Mr. Allen and myself entered and called for a glass of wine. I drank a glass in haste, but unfortunately had no small change, and this circumstance alone prevented my worthy friend from going with me. I hastily told him I would cross the little square in front, turn the first corner and there wait for him to join me. I then slipped out of the shop, passed quickly over the little park, and turned the corner agreed upon, without being seen by the sergeant, while he was watching at the opposite door. I waited some minutes on the corner for Mr. Allen, and was sadly disappointed that he did not make his appearance. I had now fairly committed myself, and found I had not a moment to spare. I therefore walked with a quick step towards the Land Port Gate, not that leading to the Peninsula, but the gate situated at the N. W. extremity of the town.

My dress was a blue coat, black stock, and black cockade with an eagle in the centre. The eagle I took care to remove, and then it was *tout-a-fait* an English cockade, and I had in the whole very much the appearance of an English naval officer. I said to myself when approaching the guard at the gate, "Now is the critical moment, and the most perfect composure and consummate impudence are necessary to a successful result." I gave a stern look at the sentinel, when he returned me a respectful salute, and I was in another moment without the walls of Gibraltar.

I walked deliberately down the mole, or quay, where I was accosted by a great number of watermen offering to convey me on board my vessel. I employed one, and after getting off in the bay, he said, "Captain, which is your vessel?"

Here again I was at a loss to decide on an answer, but after gazing for a few moments on the different ships and the flags of different nations, my eye caught sight of a *galliot* with a Norwegian ensign flying, and I said to myself, "The Norwegians are a virtuous, honest people, and I am not afraid to trust them." I had been in their country, and understood the character of these hardy, honest-hearted sons of the North.

After a moment's hesitation, I replied to the boatman, "That is my vessel," pointing to the friendly *galliot*, and we were soon alongside. I jumped on board, and inquired for the captain, who soon made his appearance. I told him I had something to communicate to him. He told me to follow him into the cabin.

I immediately asked him whether he was willing to befriend a man in distress. He said, "Tell me your story, and I will try to serve you." I frankly told him I was the captain of the American letter-of-*marque* schooner lately sent into port by the frigate *Granicus,* and that I had made my escape from the garrison, and desired to get over to Algeciras as soon as possible; that I had money enough, but still I wanted his friendship, confidence and protection.

The good old gentleman had scarcely waited to hear my story to the end, before he grasped me by the hand and said, in a kind and feeling manner, "I will be your friend, I will protect you; I was once a prisoner in England, and I know what it is to be a prisoner; rest assured, my dear sir, I will do all I can to assist you."

I offered him a dollar to pay and discharge the boatman, and remained myself below in the cabin. He said, "Put up your money, I have small change, and will pay him what is just and right."

After dispatching the boatman, he returned below, and said, "Now take off your coat, and put on this large pea-jacket and fur cap."

In this costume, and with a large pipe in my mouth, I was, in less than two minutes, transformed into a regular Norwegian.

Returning again on deck, I asked my good friend the captain whether I could rely on his mate and sailors not to betray me; he said, "They are honest and perfectly trustworthy, and you need be under no apprehension on their account."

We took a social dinner together, when he observed, "I will now go on shore for an hour or two, and hear all I can about your escape, and will come back early in the evening and relate to you all I learn."

In the evening the old captain returned, pleased and delighted. He said he never saw such a hubbub as there was about town; that the whole garrison seemed to be on the lookout, that the town major, with the military and civil police, were searching every hole in Gibraltar for the captain of the American privateer; that both of my officers were put in confinement, and that the lieutenant of the frigate who had the charge of us had been arrested; in short, there was "the devil to pay," because the captain of the privateer could not be found.

The next morning I stated to my worthy friend how extremely anxious I was to go over to Algeciras, and how mortified I should be to be taken again on board the *Granicus*. He answered, "Leave that to me: I am well acquainted with a gang of smugglers who belong to Algeciras, and often sell them gin, tobacco, and other articles of trade; they will be here on board my *galliot* at 9 o'clock this evening, and will probably start for Algeciras about midnight, after they have made all their purchases; when they come I will arrange with them to take you as a passenger."

About 9 o clock that evening a long, fast-rowing boat came silently alongside, filled with men; and certainly a more desperate, villainous-looking set was never seen. Their leader and several of his men came on board the *galliot*, and after having purchased several articles and taken a glass of gin all around, the old captain inquired of the *patroon* of the boat what hour he intended to start for Algeciras, and said, that the reason of his asking the question was that his brother wanted to go to that place for a few days upon business, and he wished to engage a passage for him, and that he should be glad if his brother could lodge for a few days with his family. He answered that he should return again about midnight, and would willingly take the captain's brother, and that if he could put up with rough fare, he was welcome to stay at his house as long as he pleased. I accordingly got ready my little bundle, which consisted of a few small articles, such as a shirt or two, (for I did not forget to wear three at the time I left the *Granicus,*) and stowed it away in my hat. I agreed with my friend the Norwegian, to leave the cap and pea-jacket with the American Consul at Algeciras, to be returned to him by some safe-conveyance in the course of a few days. Agreeable to promise the boat came on board precisely at 12 o'clock, and after my friend the captain had again cautioned the *patroon* of the boat to take good care of his brother, we started.

The water in the bay was smooth, though the night was dark and favourable to the safe prosecution of the passage. The distance is about eight or ten miles from Gibraltar; and after rowing two hours, we arrived near the harbour, when we showed a light in a lantern for a minute or two, and then covered it with a jacket. This signal was repeated two or three times, until it was answered in the same way from the shore. We approached the port cautiously, and landed in silence. The *patroon* took me by the arm, and led me through many a dark winding passage. On our way we passed by several sentinels, and were frequently hailed with the shrill sound of "*Quien Viva?*" To these salutations some friendly answer was returned, and thus everything passed smoothly on, until at length we arrived at the humble dwelling of the smuggler.

In Spain, the *contrabandists* are a desperate class of men, and often spread dread and fear through a wide region of country. In many instances they are so numerous and strong that they often put the whole power of the government at defiance. The gang that brought me to Algeciras were about twenty in number, all armed to the teeth with long knives, pistols, swords, &c, and had no doubt made their arrangements during the day with the officers and sentinels who were to mount guard that night. Of course they made them a compensation in some way or other, in order that they should meet with nothing to interfere with or obstruct their nocturnal enterprises.

Early in life I had made several voyages to Spain and its colonies in America, and had acquired a pretty good knowledge of the Spanish character. I had also picked up enough of the language to enable me to make my way among them without difficulty.

There is a something about the Spaniard that immediately inspires confidence; so much so, that, although surrounded by this desperate gang of smugglers, I had not the smallest fear for my safety. It was now near 3 o'clock in the morning when we entered the small low cabin of the *patroon*. The interior consisted of one room of moderate size, with a mat hung up to serve as a partition to separate the different members of the family, which consisted of the *patroon* Antonio, his wife, and two children. The eldest, a girl, was about eight or nine years of age, and the boy a fine little fellow about six. Antonio was thirty-five or forty years old, and his wife a good-looking woman twenty-eight or thirty.

With this family I was soon placed upon the most friendly and intimate footing. A straw bed was prepared for me behind the mat screen. Before saying goodnight, Antonio told me he should leave the house very early in the morning to look after his boat and smuggled goods, and should not return until noon next day. He said his wife and little daughter would provide breakfast for me, and would purchase whatever I wished at any time. After these preliminaries were settled we all said, "*Buenas noches*," and dropped asleep.

About 7 o'clock the next morning I furnished the smuggler's wife with money to purchase bread, butter, eggs, and coffee: and when breakfast was prepared, the mother, the two children, and myself, ate our social meal together. I then took a stroll about the town of Algeciras in my Norwegian costume, and silently observed what was going on, without conversing with any person; when I entered a coffee-house I generally took a newspaper, and as I said nothing, no One appeared to notice me. I had broken the quarantine laws, and therefore deemed it prudent to keep on my disguise for a few days, and continue to live in perfect seclusion. The next night Antonio was to leave this place for Gibraltar, and by him I sent the following letter to my friend the good Norwegian.

Algeciras, Dec. 13th, 1814.

Captain of the *galliot*:

My Dear Good Friend:—I am happy to inform you that I landed here last night, or rather at 2 o'clock in the morning, and have taken up my abode in the family of our friend, the *patroon* Antonio, and now consider myself in perfect safety;—all which I owe to your kind and generous conduct. While I live my heart will ever beat with gratitude to you, my excellent friend, and if it should never be in my power to reward your disinterested kindness, I sincerely pray that God will reward and bless you and yours to the third and fourth generations. Although I live in an obscure cabin, and am here a stranger in a strange land, still I am more happy than I could possibly be in a palace, deprived of my liberty.

I shall remain here a few days in disguise, and shall be happy to receive a letter from you per Antonio. I am extremely anxious to hear what has become of my officers, and whether they have been sent prisoners to England. You said it was possible you might come over to Algeciras. I hope you will conclude to do so, and then I shall have the happiness to enjoy your society while you remain in this place.

Adieu, my dear Sir, and believe me always with esteem,

Your grateful friend,

George Coggeshall.

Antonio was absent almost all the time during the three days I remained in his family. I furnished money, and the good Maria purchased and prepared our frugal meals. When I returned from a stroll about the town, I always took care to provide cakes and *bonbons* for the children; so we soon became very good friends, and all lived very happily together, and upon terms of the most perfect equality.

After remaining here for a period of three days, I began to tire of this mode of life, and was determined to ascertain how I could get to Cadiz, where I knew I should find friends, and be farther removed from the mortifying scenes through which I had so lately passed. Accordingly, on the morning of the fourth day of my landing at Algeciras, I repaired to a café, and inquired of one of the servants whether there was an American Consul residing in the city. The boy seemed intelligent, and instantly replied that Don Horatio Sprague, the former Consul at Gibraltar, was residing here, and that he was, *un hombre de bien*. I asked for his address, when he called a boy to show me the house; so that in fifteen minutes after, I was knocking at Mr. Sprague's door, and was soon admitted into his hospitable mansion.

He was of course surprised to see a man of my appearance walk boldly into his parlour. I soon, however, explained that I was not exactly what I appeared to be: that I was an American in distress, and throwing off my great fur cap and pea-jacket, looked somewhat more like an American. I told my story, and was received and treated like a brother. He was just going to take breakfast, and said, "You will breakfast with us, and then I will send my nephew Mr. Leach with you for your bundle, and you will then return and take up your abode with me during your stay at Algeciras."

After asocial breakfast, having doffed my cap and pea-jacket, and being supplied with a hat and other articles of dress to correspond, Mr. Leach kindly accompanied me to the humble dwelling of Maria. To my great surprise, on entering the cabin, the poor woman was very distant, curtseying with profound respect, and appeared altogether like another person. The children were shy and appeared to avoid me: at first I felt hurt at the alteration, but a moment's reflection convinced me that it was quite natural, and I loved them not the less for their distant behaviour: while in my disguise they looked upon me as one of the family; but now the circumstances were changed, they regarded me in quite another light; and I felt for a moment that the artificial rules of society were chilling to a generous heart. Maria told Mr. Leach that she always thought I was a gentleman, and that she was quite happy reserve me.

After making the family suitable presents, I took my leave, promising that they should frequently see me while I remained in Algeciras, which promise I took care rigidly to fulfil.

I was now quite at home with one of the best of men, whose greatest pleasure has ever been to make others happy. His excellent nephew, William Leach, Esq., was also a fine young gentleman, and as we were all Americans together, the most perfect confidence reigned throughout this delightful family. During my stay here, I was amused with a little incident that occurred while at dinner at Mr. Sprague's table. A young English friend came over on Sunday to dine with Mr. Sprague. During dinner Mr. Sprague asked the young man what was said in Gibraltar about the captain of the American letter-of-marque having made his escape from the garrison. He said that it caused a great deal of excitement and speculation; some said the lieutenant that had charge of him was very culpable, and even insinuated that there must have been bribery connected with the business; that it was altogether a very strange affair, that a man should be able in open daylight to make his escape from Gibraltar. After answering many other questions on the subject, he wound up by saying that the captain must be a clever man, and for his part he wished him God-speed.

The young man had no suspicion that I was an American or had any connection with the business. During the conversation, whenever I caught the eye of Mr. Leach, it was with the greatest difficulty I could command my countenance. Everything, however, passed off very well, and we often joked on the subject of the honest simplicity of their young English friend.

I remained from day to day at Algeciras, anxiously waiting to hear from my two lieutenants, Messrs. Depeyster and Allen; in hopes they would by some means be able to make their escape and not be sent prisoners to England. During the daytime I used frequently to ride in the country with Mr. Sprague. In the evening we often made up an agreeable whist party, and, among other social enjoyments, my young friend Leach introduced me to two or three respectable and very agreeable Spanish families. In these families, I spent many pleasant evenings, and had my officers and crew been at liberty, I should have been quite contented and happy.

At length, after waiting at Algeciras about ten days, I learned with pain and sincere regret that all my officers and men had been sent as prisoners to England, and I now began seriously to think of leaving this place for Cadiz. There are only two ways of travelling with safety in Spain: one is *genteel* and expensive, *viz.*, with a strong guard of soldiers; the other is in simple disguise, so that no robber can feel any interest in molesting you on the road. This mode I determined to adopt.

Algeciras lies in lat. 36° 7' North, long. 5° 24' West, on the west side of Gibraltar Bay, and distant from that place by water about eight miles; whilst to go round the bay by land is about double the distance, say seventeen or eighteen miles. It contains a population of about 4,500 to 5000 souls, has a good harbour and considerable traffic. It is a very old city, and in ancient times was strongly fortified.

Mr. Sprague is a native of Massachusetts, and has long been the American Consul at Gibraltar. He is extensively known and universally beloved and respected. His house has been for many years the seat of a generous hospitality. Although he has resided so long abroad, he has not lost a particle of American feeling or the ardour of a true patriot. His nephew, Mr. William Leach, is also a worthy gentlemanly man, of superior abilities, and will ever be remembered by me with deep gratitude.

After remaining in Algeciras about a fortnight, I hired a mule and a guide to proceed with me to Cadiz. My kind friends furnished me with provisions and stores for a journey of two days. I procured a dress such as the peasants wear in this part of Andalusia, and thus prepared, on the morning of the 26th of December,

1814, I bade *adieu* to my two excellent countrymen from whom I had received so many disinterested favours.

After leaving the town we travelled about a league on a tolerably smooth road, and then turned off into a winding footpath. I was on the mule, and my guide, a merry fellow, trudged along on foot, sometimes by my side, sometimes a few yards ahead, and when we came to a smooth path I allowed him to ride on the beast behind me. The distance from Algeciras to Cadiz is about forty miles, and it was our intention to go to Medina and put up for the night. I soon found we had a very intricate and difficult journey to perform. The whole country presented a most wild and desolate appearance; in fact it seemed to me that there could have been little or no change in this part of Spain, for the last five or six centuries. There were no public roads, a very thin and scattered population that lived in a wretched state of poverty.

Sometimes we travelled through deep and dark ravines overgrown with trees and bushes: and after passing a deep and gloomy dell, where we lost sight of the sun at times for a space of half an hour, we would then commence ascending a high mountain. We generally found a time-worn footpath running in a zigzag direction up these dreary mountains. This mode of ascending would, in seaman's phrase, be called beating up.

The progress certainly is slow and fatiguing, but the traveller is richly rewarded for all his toil, when once on the top of one of these stupendous mountains. Here he has a splendid view of the Strait of Gibraltar and the broad Atlantic on the south and east, while the wild and unbroken scenery of the surrounding country is truly magnificent.

We continued to travel on in this manner until about 2 o'clock in the afternoon, when we came to a miserable *posada*. Here we stopped to feed the mule and rest and refresh ourselves for an hour, and found to my great surprise we had only made about ten miles from Algeciras, and were still about the same distance from Medina.

The people of the United States can scarcely believe that an old country like Spain, is in such a wretched condition as

I found this part of it; without roads, the land generally un-cultivated, without hotels or taverns to accommodate strangers, and infested with robbers and *banditti*; even in the vicinity of cities and large towns, there is no safety in travelling without a military guard. This is certainly a gloomy picture of poor Spain, once so great and powerful, now distracted by factions and civil war, divested of the greatest part of her once rich colonies, her government weak, without money and without credit.

There are many causes for this sad downfall, but the prin-cipal are, ignorance idleness, superstition, priest-craft, and bad government.

Oh, happy America! how glorious art thou among the na-tions of the earth! Long may an all-wise Being shower his bless-ings upon thee, and keep thee from the wiles of superstition and popery!

My guide Manuel said the mule was ready, and he only wait-ed my pleasure to proceed. I said "*Adios Señor*" to our ignorant *posadero*, and we were again wending our intricate way towards Medina. It is impossible for me to describe the windings and turnings, the uphill and down course of these villainous passage-ways I will not call them roads, for they deserve not the name.

At length we caught sight of the desired city where we were to remain during the approaching night. On beholding Medina I was forcibly struck with the beautiful simile of the Saviour's, that "a city set on a hill cannot be hid." This is literally true with respect to Medina; it stands on a high hill, its walls, churches and houses are all plastered and whitened, and it may be seen at a great distance in every direction. For about a league before we reached this elevated city we came into a more pleasant country; we now and then met with patches of cultivated and pasture land, and saw also occasionally a small *hacienda*, with running brooks and marks of civilization. In the immediate neighbour-hood of the town, I frequently saw small stone bridges, which appeared extremely ancient; they were evidently not built in modern-days, but were probably erected either by the Romans or Moors, in the olden times, when Spain was subdued by these ancient and once powerful nations. For some distance around the foot of the hill or mountain on which Medina is located, the grounds are pleasantly diversified with olive fields, orange gardens and green meadows, on which herds of cattle were grazing. When we passed through these rural scenes, the weather was soft and fine, and here we inhaled the light and exhilarating air from the orange groves. What a delightful country! God has done everything for this people, but they have done nothing for themselves. How lovely is nature when softened and cultivated by the hand of industry, and how happy is man when governed by just and righteous principles, and for the benefit of himself and his fellow-man!

Fortunately we arrived at the singular city just before sundown, which enabled me to enjoy a beautiful view from its high walls, while the sun was gilding with its setting rays the towers of the churches and the clouds and mountains beyond them. It certainly was not so grand and sublime as that which I saw in the morning from the top of the lofty mountains, but it was truly delightful to behold the peaceful scenery of pastoral life, contrasted with the wild and savage ravines in the background of the picture. Who can behold such scenes as these and not became a better man, while thus looking through nature up to nature's God? "How wonderful are thy works, O God in wisdom hast Thou made them all."

My guide led me to a miserable *posada* to put up for the night. When I asked for a room I was shown into a dark, gloomy, prison-like place about ten feet square, with a stone floor and but one chair, without a bed or a table, and all I could get from the *posadero* was a few boiled eggs, with some sour wine. Fortunately my kind friends in Algeciras had provided stores for myself and guide, so that with the eggs and wine we made a tolerable supper. Being fatigued with the day's ride, I asked for a bed, when a coarse one of straw was brought and spread upon the stone floor, without either blanket, sheet, or pillow. I threw myself upon this bed, and, with my cloak for a covering, was soon asleep, and scarcely awoke until roused at daylight by my guide to resume our journey.

Whether Manuel took me to this miserable stopping-place from motives of policy to avoid suspicion and observation, I know not. It is, however, more than probable that there are better lodging-houses for those better acquainted with the town. I had entire confidence in my guide, he being recommended by my kind friends Messrs. Sprague and Leach, and was therefore satisfied. After settling our bill, we were soon on the road descending from the lofty city. I regret I had not an opportunity of seeing more of the town, but as we had now made but half the journey, and Cadiz was still twenty-two miles distant, it was absolutely necessary to hasten our departure. I saw it was a walled town, and was told it contained about eight or ten thousand inhabitants; with a fort, or castle, two or three churches, five or six monasteries and two hospitals, and that there were several manufactories of earthenware which was principally sold in Cadiz and Seville.

After leaving Medina we found the country less mountainous and the roads tolerably good. We passed through several small towns and villages, and as we drew near to Cadiz, were able to purchase the ordinary necessaries of life. Notwithstanding we had only a journey of twenty-two miles from Medina, we did not arrive in Cadiz until 5 o'clock in the afternoon, on the 28th of December, 1814. Here I put up at one of the principal hotels for the night. The next morning I settled with and dispatched my guide; we parted mutually satisfied. I then sallied out in pursuit of my own countrymen, and soon had the good fortune to meet with an old friend, James Haggarty, Esq., a native of Richmond, Virginia.

I immediately took lodgings with that gentleman in a private family, which consisted of a widow lady and her four daughters. Señora Quartini was a native of Cadiz, and, a kind, excellent woman. The daughters were very amiable and obliging, and from their frequent intercourse with American gentlemen, two of them had acquired a pretty good knowledge of the English language. These benevolent people were full of sympathy and kindness. They were truly pious without ostentation, and although Roman Catholics, were free from bigotry. Their goodness of heart and simple manners made even strangers feel perfectly at home, and I regarded myself as fortunate in becoming an inmate of this delightful family.

My friend Haggarty introduced me to our Consul, Joseph E. Bloomfield, Esq. and also to Richard W. Mead, Esq., and his amiable family. Mr. Mead was from Philadelphia, and a resident merchant here at this time. During my stay I experienced much hospitality both from our worthy Consul and Mr. Mead. The latter gentleman politely gave me a free ticket to his box in the theatre, and rendered me many little civilities which are always gratifying to a stranger. My friend Haggarty was always ready to negotiate my drafts on Bordeaux or London, so that as far as personal comfort was concerned I had nothing to complain of. A few days after my arrival here, I received a letter from my friend William Leach, Esq., informing me that the good old Norwegian, soon after I left Algeciras, came over from Gibraltar to see me, and that he had been unable to learn the fate of my officers. The letter also brought me glad tidings of the victory of General Brown over the British, at Fort Erie, and of the prospect of an early treaty of peace, being agreed upon by the ambassadors of the two nations at Ghent.

On the first of January, 1815, I wrote to my first lieutenant, informing him of my movements since we parted at Gibraltar, and enclosed to him a supply of money and the letters of introduction so kindly given to me by Captain Wise, and Lieutenant Daly, hoping that they might be of use to him and the other officers if they were sent to England.

The Spaniards are a peculiar people, and their character can only be learned by a long residence in their country. An intelligent Spaniard prides himself more on what his country has been than on what it is at present. He mourns over its fallen greatness, and shrugs his shoulders with a sigh.

The higher classes are extremely romantic, both in love and friendship, and they consider their word fully equal to a sealed bond. This high sense of honour sometimes descends even to the highway robber; for example, I once knew a gentleman who was robbed of $400 (all the money he had with him) on the highway from Seville to Cadiz. He observed that his was a hard case, that he had not sufficient means to defray his expenses back to Cadiz.

The robber observed, "*Amigo meo,* how much will be sufficient to pay expenses on the road?"

The gentleman replied, "I think about fifteen or twenty dollars."

The robber handed him twenty dollars, with a pompous air, and drawing himself up to his full height, said, "Take it, and don't say on your return to Cadiz, that you met with a robber, who was incapable of a generous action."

The ladies also partake of the same characteristic traits; they are very effeminate and interesting, with soft and pleasing manners, and though so gentle and fascinating, are, when roused, perfect heroines in courageous action. At the time of which I am writing there was a large circus or *amphitheatre* in the vicinity of Cadiz, spacious enough to accommodate 10,000 people. I have seen the edifice filled to overflowing with all classes of the community, from the Governor and the public authorities of the town with their families, down to the common boatman and labourer; collected together to see three or four men, on foot and on horseback, fight and kill eight or ten wild bulls. When a bull has shown uncommon fury, and a corresponding degree of coolness and courage was displayed on the part of the *matadors,* I have seen this vast assemblage thrown into perfect ecstasies, and the fine ladies in, the boxes wave their white handkerchiefs with enthusiastic cries of "*Viva, Viva,*" and throw down garlands of flowers to the *matadors* in the arena.

After relating these apparent contradictions in the Spanish character, I think it will readily be conceded that it requires a long residence among them fully to understand their peculiarities. I have been for many years in communication with Spain and her colonies, and have arrived at the conclusion that there is less medium in the Spanish character, than among other nations, and that there the best and the worst people in the world are to be found.

I was living here perfectly at leisure, and what with the social intercourse of the friendly family with whom I lodged, the theatre and other public amusements, I found the time passed away pleasantly and rapidly.

On the 14th, of January, I received a warm-hearted letter from my kind and ever obliging friend Horatio Sprague, in which he mentioned that my escape had been the wonder of Gibraltar, that an unremitted search was made for me during three days, both in the city and among the vessels in the bay, and that the noble old Norwegian was fairly infested with midshipmen and others searching after me. Although I was agreeably located in Cadiz, and found many kind friends from whom I had received much hospitality and friendly favours, still I was an idler, and began to tire of such an inactive, useless life, and as there was no prospect of obtaining a passage home from this place, I decided to take passage in a small Portuguese schooner for Lisbon. This was a coasting vessel, manned with a captain, mate and ten men, just double the number of men that would be employed to navigate an American vessel of the same size. In this schooner I agreed for a berth in the cabin, and was to furnish my own stores, with the *proviso*, that the cook should likewise do all the cooking I might require. With this understanding I purchased a few hams, a bag of bread, a demijohn of wine, tea, sugar, coffee, and other stores sufficient for fifteen days.

The schooner being ready, I bade *adieu* to all my friends in Cadiz on the 15th of February, 1815, having been there just forty-nine days. I sailed out of the bay with a heavy heart at parting with so many who were true and faithful. I had a few choice books with me to read on the passage, and had become so much accustomed to all kinds of life, that I felt I should be able to accommodate myself to almost any condition. I soon found that the captain was a good disciplinarian and managed his vessel very well. Although he had never made a foreign voyage, he knew the coast and understood his business, and I felt myself fortunate in having fallen into such good hands.

This was the first time I had ever sailed under the Portuguese flag, and many of their customs were quite new to me. One peculiarity I observed that I never witnessed before.

Three times a day the captain summoned everybody on board to the quarter deck; then they all knelt down, morning, noon, and evening, and repeated their prayers, the captain always taking the lead. The schooner was a dull sailer, and as we had generally light winds we did not reach Cape St. Vincent until the fifth day after leaving Cadiz. This is a high, bold cape, lying in lat. 37° 3' North, long 9° 2' West.

We passed close to this conspicuous headland, I should think not more than half a mile distant, on the 20th of February, at 4 o'clock in the afternoon, when the captain called all hands to the quarter deck and addressed them as follows:

Officers and men, it has pleased God to bring us in safety thus far on our voyage; now let us all kneel down and thank him for his goodness and mercy to us poor sinners, and beseech him to conduct us in safety to our destined port.

They were, I should think, some fifteen or twenty minutes occupied in prayer, and then returned to their ordinary vocations.

We crept slowly along shore, and on the 23rd of February got safe into Lisbon, after a passage of eight days. I regret that I recollect neither the captain's name nor that of his vessel. I had made so many voyages to this place that upon landing I felt quite at home, and was soon in the society of many of my own countrymen. I met in Lisbon a New York friend, James L. Kennedy, Esq., who came out to that place supercargo of an American vessel, and was, like myself, very desirous of returning, to New York. Mr. Kennedy, during his stay in Lisbon, became acquainted with a Portuguese house in the wine trade. These gentlemen owned a nice little brig of about one hundred and eighty tons burthen, called the *Tres Hermanos*. They loaded her with a cargo of wine, oil, &c, and agreed with him to proceed in her to New York as supercargo, with liberty to return again to Lisbon in the brig or remain in New York, whichever should suit his interest. She was commanded by a very young man with but little experience, and had a miserable set of Portuguese sailors. In this brig one of the owners offered me a passage free from any charge, upon condition that I would assist the young captain with my experience and advice. He had never been to the United States, and said he should be very happy to profit by my experience. My friend Kennedy was also very desirous that I should go, and said we should enjoy each other's society, and that would shorten the passage. I must confess I had some serious misgivings on the subject of sailing under the Portuguese flag with an inefficient captain and a filthy crew, but as there was no American vessel to sail for several weeks, and the treaty of peace with Great Britain was not ratified, I concluded to take passage in this neutral vessel.

Before sailing, the principal owner told the captain to attend to the comfort of Mr. Kennedy and myself, and to treat us with respect, and consult me always on the most judicious course to steer, &c. &c. He promised to comply with the request of the owner, and with much complacency said he had no doubt we should be very happy together. All these promises he most shamefully broke a few days after we got to sea. I remained in Lisbon just eighteen days, and, on the 13th of March, 1815, sailed in the good brig *Tres Hermanos* for New York.

After getting to sea I was determined not to interfere with the course of the vessel, nor to proffer my advice unless it was called for, and then with the greatest delicacy, and never in the slightest degree made any remark to offend the mates or sailors during the long and tedious passage. The little, narrow-minded captain did not consult me at all on the course of the vessel, and absolutely appeared so jealous of me that my position was almost insupportable, and had not my friend Kennedy been on board, and the brig bound to New York, I should probably have been

104

worse treated by these wretches. Although I scarcely exchanged a word with one of his men during the passage, I once overheard them say they should like to knock, me in the head and throw me overboard. In lieu of steering a judicious course and keeping a fair distance to the northward of the Western Islands, the poor devil steered down among the islands, where we were becalmed for several days and made miserable progress getting to the westward. The brig was in such a filthy condition that Mr. Kennedy and myself suffered out of measure with one of the plagues of Egypt. The probability is, that before leaving Lisbon the sailors were allowed to sleep in the berths in the cabin, and thus every part of the vessel was overrun with vermin.

By contrary winds and bad management, our passage was prolonged to fifty-eight days. On the 9th of May we took a Sandy Hook pilot, and the same day arrived in New York. I was rejoiced to land once more in the United States, after an absence of sixteen months and twenty-one days.

I cannot leave this brig, without warning my friends and countrymen never to take passage across the Atlantic in a Portuguese vessel of any description.

On my return home I found all my family and friends well. Peace was again restored to the United States.

Seven and a half months after this date, I received a letter from Mr. Henry Allen, a worthy young man, who was second lieutenant with me in the *Leo*, from which I make the following extracts:—

Salem, December 24th, 1815.

Captain George Coggeshall;

Dear Sir:—If you have seen Mr. Depeyster, he has probably informed you of my unfortunate attempt to escape from Gibraltar.

After waiting about ten minutes, (time I thought sufficient for you to reach the mole,) I left the wine shop in the same manner as yourself, and had already passed the two gates, and was on the mole, when I was arrested by the sergeant under whose charge we were, who demanded, in the most severe manner, where you were. Sensible that you must have been on the mole at the time, I told him that when you left me, you were going to Messrs. Turnbull & Co.'s. He immediately turned back, and with myself proceeded to their house. After gaining it, and passing away about forty-five minutes, he suspected I was deceiving him, consequently returned with me to the mole to make all inquiries, but in vain. He left your description with the officer of the mole. He then dragged me to the town major, who went immediately on horseback to every passage in the garrison with your description.

Fortune and my best wishes favoured your escape, however. We were carried to England and remained till the 29th of April, then released, and I came home as an agent for one of the Cartels.

CHAPTER 5

Voyage in the Ship *John Hamilton*

A few days after my arrival at New York, in the Portuguese brig *Tres Hermanos*, from Lisbon, I returned to my quiet home at Milford, Connecticut, on a visit to my family and friends, and was most happy in again meeting with those so dear to my heart, after an absence during which I had passed through such changes and perils. I felt truly grateful to God for having delivered me from the power of the enemy and the violence of the tempest. Soon, however, to my great regret, I received a letter from my former employers, Archibald Gracie & Sons, requesting me to come down to New York.

During our war with Great Britain (which had but recently terminated), a large English ship called the *John Hamilton* was captured by some American cruiser, sent into Baltimore, and there condemned with her cargo. This ship was 533 tons burthen, and laden with mahogany from the Bay of Honduras, and bound for England. American papers were obtained for her, and Messrs. Gracie &. Sons became her agents. By their request I left New York for Baltimore on the 9th of June, 1815, to take the command and proceed from Baltimore to Savannah, for a cargo of rice and cotton for Lisbon. I agreed with Mr. Charles M. Hanstrom to go with me in the capacity of chief mate: Mr. Hanstrom had been formerly mate with me in the ship *America,* and was a very worthy, efficient man.

He left New York a few days after, and joined the ship in Baltimore. I took also with me my youngest brother Francis, a lad about seventeen years old, as my clerk, and sent him to Baltimore by water in charge of my baggage. I arrived at Baltimore on the 12th of June, and took charge of the ship. She had been laid up for several months, and upon examination I found the fore and main masts quite rotten, and many other spars of less importance, also defective. These masts and spars were all replaced with new ones, and the ship calked and ballasted with stone, before she could proceed to sea.

This occupied about a month, when I shipped a second mate, Mr. Archibald R. Gracie, of Jamaica, L. I., a fine young man about twenty-two years of age, with a crew of fifteen seamen; and on the 12th of July left Baltimore, bound for Savannah. We had light winds from the southward, and did not leave the Capes until the 17th. I discharged the pilot off Cape Henry. The ship was in light ballast trim, only drawing eleven feet water, and when the wind was ahead we made but little progress beating to windward.

It was now midsummer, the weather extremely warm, and the winds light and almost, constantly ahead, from the S. W., so that with the greatest exertion we were not able to pass Cape Hatteras until the tenth day after leaving Cape Henry, and day after day were beating with light winds from the southward and westward, in sight of Cape Fear. It was one of the most tedious passages I ever made considering the short distance.

We however arrived safe at Savannah on the 7th of August, after a passage of twenty-five days. The summer, up to this date, had been excessively hot, and the winds almost constantly from the S. W. Many vessels from the northern States had long passages as well as ourselves. One ship was fifty-four days in reaching there from New York.

The *John Hamilton* leaked so badly on the passage, that I did not think it prudent to take a cargo on board without calking her bottom, and for this purpose was compelled to heave her out and calk her throughout; this occupied about ten days. The ship drew too much water to load at the town, and we were obliged to drop her several miles down the river, to a place called "Four-mile Point," to take the cargo on board. Our consignee, or commercial agent there, was Barney McKinney, Esq. This gentleman had purchased a cargo of rice and cotton, by order and for account of Francis T. Sampayo, Esq., a Portuguese gentleman, at this time residing in New York. It had been ready to go on board for several weeks, but owing to our detention, refitting the ship in Baltimore, long passage, and heaving out to repair, combined, we were delayed until the midst of the sickly season.

A few days after we commenced taking in the cargo, several of the sailors were taken sick with the yellow fever. Three out of five that I put into the hospital died in a few days, and this so alarmed the others, when taken ill, that they begged me, for God's sake, not to send them there to die, as their shipmates had done, but to get board for them in a private family. Accordingly, I hired a small house for their accommodation, and got a physician and black nurses to attend them. Though the poor fellows were better attended to, still several of them died; and not one of the crew escaped sickness, except the cook and steward. I was obliged to hire negroes to take on board and stow away the cargo.

On the 1st of September, Mr. Hanstrom was taken sick with the fever. I had him brought on shore, and placed him in a private family, and hired a physician and a nurse to attend him. The next day the second mate, Mr. Gracie, was taken to the same house, very ill with the fever, as was also my brother Francis; so that both mates and my brother were very ill in one house, and the sailors in another.

I was therefore obliged, myself, to attend to sending the cargo on board, besides visiting the sick in both houses. In consequence of this severe duty, watching at night with my brother, and the two mates, and the exposure to the sun during the day, I was also taken very ill of the fever, at the hotel where I resided. I had once had the yellow fever in Martinique, and knew the necessity of taking powerful medicine in the first stage of the disease. Accordingly, I acted as my own physician, and in two days after was able to visit the sick in both houses again.

Poor Gracie, the second mate, died on the 12th of September, after ten days' illness.

Mr. Hanstrom lingered until the 19th of the same month, when he died.

My brother Francis was extremely reduced, and narrowly escaped death; in fact, he was so feeble and emaciated, that when the ship was ready for sea I was obliged to leave him in the family of a friend, to be sent home so soon as he should be able to endure the fatigue of the passage to New York.

This was the most sickly season that had been known for many years, so that when an English ship was announced, and an inquiry was made as to whom she was consigned, the reply was, that the ship and cargo were consigned to A., B. & Co., but the captain and crew were consigned to Old Watts (the undertaker).

I have always found that in very sickly places, when men are surrounded with the dead and dying, that danger and death make but little impression on the minds of survivors, and produce little or no solemnity, so quickly do they become hardened and callous to the sufferings of their fellows. During the summer there were three or four English ships here, which lost their captains, officers, and nearly all their men, and their consignees were not able to dispatch the vessels until the winter months. The merchants thought me fortunate in getting away in what they termed so short a time. My ship was loaded with 1,393 *tierces* of rice, and 638 bales of cotton, and it was now my first duty to obtain officers and men. I found it impossible to get a suitable chief mate, and was therefore obliged to take the best I could find, who was a Mr. Peleg Billings, a native of New London, Connecticut. Mr. Billings had been reared to the sea in a fishing-smack; he was a good-natured, honest man, and, for aught I know, a very good fisherman, but no more fit for chief mate of such a ship, than I was to be the pope of Rome.

I appointed a second mate from among the seamen. His name was William Norton. He had never before been an officer, and was a man without any pretensions, but in the main was a pretty good fellow.

With these two mates, a Dutch carpenter, cook, and steward, and three or four of the old crew, who had escaped death but were still weak from the effects of sickness, I took the ship down near the mouth of the river, and repaired to the town and picked up such men as I could find that were willing to ship for a voyage to Lisbon. After a day or two I succeeded in getting six seamen, of all nations; and such as they were, I was compelled to pay them twenty-five dollars per month, and to the chief mate fifty. After becoming ready for sea, the wind continued for several days to blow a strong gale from the N. E., with rainy, dark weather, and we were unable to get out until the morning of the 3rd of October. At meridian, this day, the light-house on Tybee Island bore west, six miles distant. At 2 discharged the pilot, the light-house bearing N. W., twelve or fourteen miles distant. Several of the sailors were still sick, but nearly all of them convalescent.

Tybee Light-house lies in lat. 32° 00' N.; long. 80° 42' W. of London.

Oct. 4th.—Strong gales from N. E. and E. N. E. throughout all these 24 hours, with little or no current, as we were inside of the gulf stream.

Oct. 5th.—Moderate breezes from the eastward during the whole of these 24 hours. I found the current setting N. E. two and a half miles the hour. Lat. by obs. 31° 51' N.; long, per account, 79° 36'.

Oct. 6th.—Light winds from the eastward throughout these 24 hours. Lat. by obs. 32° 8' N.

Oct. 7th and 8th.—Light airs and calm weather; gained very little, and nothing transpired worth remarking.

Oct. 10th.—Strong gales from the south and S. W., attended by severe squalls and rain. Lat. by obs. 34° 37' N.; long, per account 75° 5' W.

Oct. 11th.—Brisk breezes from the southward throughout these 24 hours.

Oct. 12th and 13th.—Light airs from the northward, In the afternoon of the 13th, passed near a ship standing to the westward, with loss of main and mizzen-mast. She required no assistance.

Oct. 14th.—Passed near a ship standing to the southward.

Oct. 15th.—Moderate breezes from the E. S. E.; no incident occurred worth remarking. Lat. by obs. 37° 19' North.

Oct. 16th.—First part of these 24 hours light winds and calm. At 4 a. m. stiff gales at E. N. E., double reefed the top-sails, dark, cloudy weather. Lat. by obs. 37° 26' North.

Oct. 17th.—Strong gales from the E. N. E. throughout all these 24 hours, attended with showers of rain. Ship making much water. Lat. by obs. 37° 52' North.

Oct. 18th.—First and middle part of these 24 hours strong gales. At 8 p. m. hove to with the ship's head to the N. E. Wind E. by S. and E. S. E. and a high sea running. Lat. by obs. 39° 8' North.

Oct. 19th.—Strong gales from the E. N. E. and N. E. At 2 p. m. made sail to the S. E., strong gales and rainy weather; at midnight hove to under a close reefed main-top-sail and lay until 8 a. m. when we again made sail; saw a ship to the westward standing S. E.; ship leaking very much. One pump almost constantly employed. Pumped up much rice, and being now in great distress, with the chief mate and ten men sick below, I judged it best to steer for New York. I accordingly bore up and ran to the westward. In consequence of the illness of the chief mate and so many of the crew, I was obliged to keep the deck almost day and night. Lat. 38° 56' N.; long, about 69° W.

Oct. 20th.—Strong gales at E. and E. N. E. Still standing to the westward. Ship leaking badly; one pump going nearly all the time and pumping up much rice. The ship laboured and strained to such a degree, that many of the ground tier casks were crushed and broken, so that the pumps were often choked with loose rice, and as the ship had a very flat floor, it often happened that the water would lie in the bilge of the ship, so that I was frequently obliged to keep her off before the wind, to free her from water in order to prevent the ground tier from being damaged. The latter part of these 24 hours the wind moderated and the weather became much better.

Oct. 21st.—Light winds and variable, with dark cloudy weather; made but little progress to the westward; ship still leaking badly; from eight to ten men unfit for duty; latter part of the 24 hours light winds and variable. Lat. by obs. 38° 13' N., long, per account, about 71° 44' W.

Oct. 22nd.—These 24 hours commenced with brisk breezes from the northward and westward; found it impossible to get to the westward, when I again bore up and ran to the eastward, determined to make the best of my way to Lisbon. Lat. by obs. 39° 20' N.

Oct. 23rd.—Moderate breezes from the westward and open cloudy weather; still steering to the eastward, carrying all the sail I could do with safety: eight men sick below, and the chief mate unable to keep the deck. Lat. by obs. 39° 43' N., long. 70° W.

Oct. 24th and 25th.—Strong gales from the westward throughout these two days; still running to the eastward. Lat. at noon 39° 43' N.

Oct. 26th.—These 24 hours commenced with strong gales at S. W. and a high sea running. At 8 p. m. carried away the maintop-mast, just above the cap, strong gales at S. W. and W. S. W. with a high sea running, weather very dark and squally; both mates and ten men sick below; both pumps employed nearly all the time, and almost constantly choking with rice. I was unable to leave the deck during the whole night. I have often seen hard times at sea, but this night was the worst. Four good and true men with the cook and steward were all I could muster during

SHIP *JOHN HAMILTON* IN A GALE OCT. 26TH 1815

the whole of this dreadful night. Toward the end of these 24 hours, the weather became a little more moderate. No obs.; lat. by account 39° 43' N.; long. 61° 22' W.

Oct. 27th.—Strong gales from the S. W., with much sea; got the heel of the main-top-mast on deck, and cleared away the wreck. The chief mate and eight men still below, and unable or unwilling to come on deck. Ship still leaking very much. Lat. by obs. 41° 34' N.; long. 44° 0' W.

Oct. 28th.—Fresh breezes from the westward; now making very good progress to the eastward; although the maintop-mast was gone, we ran on our course at a fast rate; set the carpenter at fitting and getting ready a new main–top-mast. Lat. by obs. 41° 34' N.; long. 56° 10' W.

Oct. 29th.—These twenty-four hours commenced with strong breezes from the S. W., with rain; latter part more moderate. At 9 a. m. spoke the ship *Sachem,* Captain Davis, of New York, twenty-seven days from Bordeaux, bound home. Captain Davis kindly offered to render me any assistance in his power, but as the wind was favourable, I thanked him for his politeness and made what sail I could, and stood on our course. Lat. by account 42° 24' N.

Oct. 30th.—Moderate breezes from the westward and fine weather. This day I was compelled to perform a most disagreeable duty, that of punishing one of my men, the Dutch carpenter, whose violation and gross insubordination of language and manner, especially when my situation was most critical and perilous, were such as to leave me no alternative but that of making an example of him, or of abandoning all discipline. He was of quick and fiery temper, and had in some way obtained liquor, and with its added fury became a most dangerous man. He foamed at the mouth, but after being severely chastised, and being literally drenched with water, which I found it necessary to have thrown upon him to cool him, he became orderly and continued so during the rest of the voyage.

Oct. 31st.—Light winds from the N.W. and fine weather; ship leaking badly; six men still unable to do duty; the two mates were able to be on deck only in fine weather. Lat. by obs. 41° 20'; long. 50° 41' W.

Nov. 1st.—At 6 a. m. one of the sick seamen died. After suffering for several weeks, he gradually declined, and finally expired apparently without a struggle. He was an elderly man, of a mild and gentle temper. I shipped him in Savannah, just before sailing.

Nov. 2nd.—This day moderate breezes from the E. N. E., and fine weather. At noon got up the new main-top-mast; passed near a brig standing to the westward; in the afternoon committed the body of the deceased seaman to the great deep with the usual solemnities. These twenty-four hours end with light winds from the eastward and fine weather.

Nov. 3rd and *4th.*—Moderate breezes from the S.W. and open cloudy weather; nothing worth remarking occurred during the last two days.

Nov. 5th.—At 6 a. m. made the Island of Corvo, bearing south twelve or fifteen leagues distant; middle and latter part of these twenty-four hours light winds from the northward and fine weather. Lat. by obs. 40° 34' N.; long 31° 5' W.

Nov. 6th and *7th.*—Moderate breezes and variable, with open cloudy weather; on the 7th at noon, lat. 39° 46' N.

Nov. 8th.—Light winds and variable; at meridian saw the island of Terceira bearing south eight or ten leagues distant. Lat. by obs. 39° 24' N.; long. 27° 12' W.

Nov. 9th.—We still had a continuation of light winds and fine weather.

Nov. 10th.—We still had a continuation of fine weather; another of the sick men who had suffered with the yellow fever in Savannah expired from its effects.

Nov. 11th.—In the afternoon of this day committed the body of poor Williams, the seaman, to its watery grave. It was a sad and solemn scene. Lat. 40° 11' N.; long. 26° W.

The remainder of the passage was a repetition of the same light winds, and generally fine weather, which contributed to restore the officers and seamen to a better state of health.

Nov. 21st.—We got safe into Lisbon, after a passage of forty-six days, and I think I can safely say the most disagreeable one I ever made, up to this period of my life.

We came to anchor nearly opposite Belem Castle, and in consequence of bad weather remained there for several days. My ship and cargo were consigned to H. T. Sampayo, a rich merchant established in Lisbon, and a gentleman of great influence with all the public authorities, which I suppose was the reason I escaped from quarantine.

On my arrival, my officers and crew so far recovered as to pass inspection tolerably well. On the 23rd of November we moved the ship farther up the river, nearly opposite to the town, and as the cotton was transshipped to England, we were allowed to discharge it forthwith into two small English brigs. This facilitated our unloading, and made clear room to discharge the rice.

On the 27th instant, while I was on shore, a very unpleasant affair occurred on board. Mr. Norton, the second mate, had some difficulty with an ordinary seaman belonging to the interior of Georgia, when the sailor, in a fit of passion, drew from his pocket a small knife, and stabbed him in his left side. When I came on board in the evening, I found the poor fellow in great distress. For some hours I feared the wound would prove mortal; fortunately, however, the knife had not penetrated far, and in a few days he was able to resume his duty. The man who inflicted the wound appeared very humble and penitent, and with the consent and advice of Mr. Hutchinson, the American consul, I forthwith discharged him. He returned to Savannah, and here the business ended.

After the cotton was discharged, we commenced landing a portion of the rice. As there was no voyage determined on, there appeared to be no hurry on the part of the consignee, and we had merely to land the rice from time to time, when sold. A survey was held on the ship, and it was found necessary to heave her out, re-calk and copper her with new copper. The second mate, and almost all the seamen, desired to be discharged, and as it was uncertain whither she would proceed after leaving Lisbon, an arrangement was made with the men, with the consent of the American consul, that they should be discharged and paid off.

Accordingly, about the first of January, Mr. Norton, the second mate, and nearly all the crew, were discharged and left the ship, after which I hired men by the day to discharge the cargo. Towards the last of January, when the greatest part of the rice was landed, we found that a large portion of the ground tier was badly damaged with salt water, I think from one hundred and thirty to one hundred and fifty casks. Had the *John Hamilton* been built in the United States, little or none of the rice would have been damaged. I think the construction of merchant ships in the United States is far better than in England. Many of the ports in England are quite dry at low water, and their ships must be built quite flat on the bottom, so that they will not heel when aground at low water; whereas, in North America, it is not necessary to build our ships to take the ground, there being very few "tide harbours" in the United States.

The *John Hamilton* was built at Whitby, England, and was exceedingly flat on the floor, and whenever I carried taut sail upon the wind, the water would lie in the lee bilge where the pumps would not reach it. Often, on the passage out, I was obliged to keep the ship off before the wind to pump her out, and after every possible care was taken to prevent it, still a great portion of the ground tier of rice was badly damaged. Sharp built ships are not liable to this evil, and in my opinion sail faster and work better than the merchant ships built in England.

While in Lisbon I took lodgings on the third floor of a large stone building five stories high. The family with whom I lived was composed of two widow ladies, sisters. One of these ladies had four children, the eldest a girl of thirteen years, the youngest about four years old. On the night of the 1st of February, at one hour after midnight, I was awaked from a profound sleep by a violent earthquake, and before I had time to dress, the whole family came rushing into my room in their nightclothes, crying, "*O! Dios Misericordia. Misericordia; Don Gorge Misericordia.*" The women were alarmed almost to distraction, the children were crying, dogs barking, and the chairs and tables rattling about the room; while the immense stone edifice in which we lived was reeling to and fro, apparently in the act of tumbling to the ground. I called for a light, which after some moments was brought, and thanks be to God the earth had then ceased to quake. There were various opinions about its duration, some affirmed that it lasted two minutes, others that it lasted but one; I think the truth lay between the extremes.

Had it continued a minute or two longer, I have no doubt the greatest part of the city would have been thrown down. Soon after the alarm had in some measure subsided, I threw open the window and found the weather was dark and cloudy, with a little rain, but no wind. About 6 o'clock in the morning we experienced a second shock. This shock, although very severe, only lasted a few seconds, and passed off without doing any damage. The next morning the whole city was in a high state of excitement; nearly all the pendulum clocks in the town had stopped. Many of the houses were cracked and very much injured. Every person I met had something to relate about the convulsion. That night there was a grand ball of ladies and gentlemen. They had ceased dancing and had just seated themselves at the supper table, when the earth began to shake. A gentleman who was present told me it was a most distracting scene; he said the dishes and glasses were dancing about the table, and many of them thrown on the floor and broken. Some of the ladies fainted, others were ringing their hands, and crying for help, while "*Misericordia,*" resounded from every part of the grand saloon.

The priests, as is usual on such occasions, wished to turn this great convulsion of nature to their own account; they told the people it was sent in punishment for their sins, and advised universal confession, fasting, and prayer. For some eight or ten days after this great event almost every vessel that arrived had sensibly felt the earthquake; some at a distance of at least 400 miles from the port. Letters received from Oporto, stated that it was very severely felt in that city, and I have no doubt but the whole of this little kingdom experienced more or less of the convulsion.

A few days after this happened I had a conversation with Mr. John Caffery of this place, on the subject of earthquakes. Mr. Caffery was a worthy, intelligent, elderly gentleman of English parentage, and was then about seventy-one years of age. He told me that he witnessed the horrors of the great earthquake in 1755, that he was then a boy of ten years of age, and with his father visited many parts of the city. He said it occurred between 10 and 11 o'clock in the morning, that great numbers of the people fled from their dwellings and that many of the houses took fire; crowds of people rushed into the churches for greater safety, when, sad to relate, the churches were thrown down, and thousands crushed to death in the ruins. He pointed out to me the location of a great stone mole or quay where at the time a ferry was kept; it was a thoroughfare where throngs of people collected to pass to the opposite side of the river. In an instant the whole of this vast quay disappeared and every person perished, and to use his own words, not a hat or bonnet was seen floating on the surface; and on the same spot where this stupendous quay sunk, was found three or four fathoms of water.

To fill up the measure of sickness and death during this disastrous voyage, I will here relate another melancholy circumstance that occurred while lying here. Before leaving Baltimore, I shipped a carpenter by the name of George Patterson, a native of Norfolk, Virginia. This man was extremely sick nearly all the time we remained at Savannah, but by great care and good nursing, he so far recovered as to be able to proceed on the voyage.

In consequence of the low state of Patterson's health, I shipped the insubordinate Dutchman to act as carpenter until Patterson should be able to do his duty. He however continued ill the greatest part of the passage out, but on our arrival got quite well.

He was a tall man, six feet two inches in height, and large in proportion, of an amiable temper, and in every respect a good man, and an excellent carpenter. Before heaving the ship down I had several calkers employed on her upper works while she was lying at anchor in the Tagus, nearly opposite Lisbon. These men were at work on stages hung over the side of the ship, and Patterson among the number, when at 8 o'clock in the morning of the 13th of February, the order was given for all hands to leave off work and take breakfast. Patterson lingered behind as I suppose to finish a thread of oakum, and all the men went to breakfast. I came on deck about ten or fifteen minutes after and inquired for the carpenter, but alas! he was not to be found, nor was he ever seen or heard of from that time. The current in the river at this time was running very strong, and the probability is, that the poor fellow slipped off the stage and sunk to rise no more. How inscrutable are the designs of Providence; this man who had escaped death in so many shapes from the yellow fever, and the tempest, now when in apparent safety was snatched into eternity in a moment.

After the cargo was all discharged, the ship was hove down, calked, and coppered. A voyage to the East Indies was projected, and some preparations were made towards it, but for some cause or other it was finally abandoned, and after lying in Lisbon about four months and a half, I was ordered to ballast the ship with salt, to go to St. Ubes and take on board the balance of a cargo of the same article, and proceed thence to New York. I accordingly shipped a new crew, who put on board 200 *moyes* of salt, and on the 7th of April 1816 I left Lisbon, and after a passage of six hours got safe at anchor at St. Ubes. The ship was consigned to Messrs. Rego & Sons, to procure a cargo for account of Francis T. Sampayo, Esq. Our consignee gave me good dispatch, so that in nine days I took on board 600   of salt and was ready for sea. A few days before sailing, Frederick Beal, Esq., came here from Lisbon and took passage with me for New York.

Mr. Beal was a native of Stockholm, Sweden, and was a gentlemanly man, very companionable, and altogether an agreeable passenger. After loading the ship with salt she drew seventeen feet water, and as the channel at the mouth of the harbour was very narrow and at this time neap tides, I was obliged to wait several days for a fair wind and spring tides before I could pass the bar. After waiting until the 24th of April we left St. Ubes, bound for New York. It being a fine season of the year we met with nothing worth remarking for many days, and when we had wind enough to steady the ship we got on pretty well, but when the sea was high and the winds light the ship rolled terribly, with a short jerking motion, so that I was in constant fear of losing the top-mast, notwithstanding I had the greatest bulk of the cargo in the centre, and a large portion of the salt raised high up between decks. In a calm, when the sea was high, it was to me perfect torture to watch the masts, expecting at every roll to see the top-masts go over the side. This was owing to the bad construction of the ship.

We worked our way to the westward without any incident worth remarking, until the 18th of May. At daylight we fell in with a great number of ice islands, many of which were enormously large; several of them I think from 70 to 80 feet above the water, and from 150 to 200 feet long. The weather being fine, I went in the yawl to the leeward of one of these immense islands, and took lines with me with the intention of ascending to the top of one of the highest of them, and if possible to measure the exact height, but when I came to examine the mass, I found so much sea washing and dashing up against its sides that it was impossible to ascend it; and although a portion of the top of the islands was porous ice and snow, near the water and for several yards above the surface it was as smooth as glass, and dangerous and difficult, if not impossible to ascend. Lat. by obs. at noon 43° 24' N.; long, by a good lunar obs. 51° 58' W.

May 23rd.—At 9 a. m. made the island of Sable, bearing W. S. W. about three or four leagues distant, at the same time saw a fishing schooner at anchor. We had no observation of the sun, it being obscured by clouds and fog; wind from the E. N. E. To clear the island we hauled to the southward. After leaving the island of Sable we continued to work along to the westward, and generally had fine weather until the 30th of May, when we arrived at New York all well after a passage of thirty-one days from St. Ubes.

I remained in New York a few days, and after I had discharged the crew, returned home to Milford. This has been altogether the most anxious and fatiguing voyage I ever made. I found all my family and friends well, and after remaining about a week at my mother's house, returned to New York and attended to discharging the salt. It was a large cargo, I think 18,300 bushels. I then resigned the command of the *John Hamilton,* with a fixed determination to remain on shore for several months, and again returned to my native home in Milford on the 15th of June.

CHAPTER 6

Voyage in the Pilot-Boat Schooner
Sea Serpent

After having settled the last voyage I made in the *Volusia* from New Orleans to Truxillo and Bonaco, and disposed of that vessel, I decided to make up a voyage to the Pacific. By recent accounts from Peru we learned that Lord Cochran, with a Chilean fleet, was blockading Lima, aided by a strong land force under the command of General St. Martin; that the Spaniards had concentrated their armies in Lima and its vicinity, and had strongly fortified themselves there and at the castles of Callao, and would probably hold out for at least six months longer. We also heard that the inhabitants of Lima were in great want of everything, especially provisions of almost every description. On the receipt of this information Mr. H., a merchant of New York, proposed to me in the month of October, 1821, to purchase a fast-sailing pilot-boat schooner and fit her out for Lima, with a view of evading the blockade, and profiting by the high prices which could be obtained for almost everything sent to that place.

We soon made arrangements to purchase a suitable vessel, to be owned by Mr. H., Mr. B., an Italian gentleman and myself. I agreed to take one fifth interest in the schooner and cargo, and to command the vessel, and act as supercargo during the voyage. The enterprise was well planned, and had the cargo been laid in with good judgement, the voyage would have proved eminently successful. As it was managed by Mr. H. and Mr. B. it proved in the end rather a failure.

I had never been in Lima and knew nothing of its wants; Mr. B. had resided there several years, but as he was not a merchant, his information proved of little service. I relied entirely on the judgement of my two associates, and therefore took many articles not at all adapted to the market. Such articles as were wanted at Lima paid an enormous profit,

After searching about for a week or two, we at length found a sharp pilot-boat built schooner called the *Sea-Serpent*. Her burthen was 139 tons. Though only three years old, she was soft and defective, and subsequently proved to be rotten, and, in bad weather, very leaky. The schooner had just returned from a voyage to Chagrés, where she had lost her captain and officers and nearly all her crew by the yellow fever, and while in that hot climate she was not properly ventilated, and had thus suffered from dry rot.

The defect was not discovered by the carpenter who was sent to examine her before she was purchased by Mr. H. I think we gave seven thousand five hundred dollars for the schooner, and on or about the 20th of October we commenced loading. We first took in ten or twelve tons of English and Swedish iron and 100 flasks of quicksilver, which cost over $3,500. Six hogsheads containing 234 kegs of butter, about 2,500 pounds, and other articles of French, English and German goods, not at all adapted to the market, situated as the people of Lima were, in the midst of war and threatened with famine.

The whole cost of the vessel and cargo, including the insurance out, was $30,726.

Mr. B.'s interest amounted to $5,000, my own was one fifth of the adventure, and the remainder belonged to Mr. H. I subsequently, before sailing, sold to my friend Richard M. Lawrence, Esq., of New York, half of my interest in both vessel and cargo, leaving for my account only about $3,000. Beside this amount, I had, however, for my own private adventure about $1,500 in jewellery and silk stockings. These articles, though valuable, occupied but a very small space in the stowage of the vessel. I took with me Mr. B. as passenger, my cousin Mr. Freegift Coggeshall as chief mate, my brother Francis Coggeshall as second mate, and a crew of nine men and boys, including the cook and steward.

Thus loaded and manned, we sailed from New York, on the 15th of November, 1821, for Lima. For the first and second days out we had fine weather and fair winds from the westward. On the third day, November 17th, we met with strong gales from the eastward and a high head sea running, so that we were compelled to lay to ten or twelve hours. Our decks were filled with water and the schooner began to leak, which was a bad sign at the commencement of a long voyage. The next day the wind shifted to the westward, when we again made sail and stood on our course to the eastward. We continued to have strong gales from the westward and very bad weather until the 4th of December, when we made the Island of St. Mary's, bearing E. S. E. five leagues distant. This is one of the Azores or Western Islands, and lies in lat. 36° 59′ North, long. 25° 10′ West.

We lost here two days, by reason of strong gales from the S. S. W., with a high head sea, and very squally weather. After getting into lat. 24° N., we took the regular trade winds, and generally had pleasant weather; but whenever we encountered a strong breeze, we found the schooner leaked considerably, and being deeply laden, she was extremely wet and uncomfortable.

On the night of the 17th of December, 1821, when in lat. 16°, long, about 25° W., we caught fifty-eight flying-fish on deck. The schooner was so deep and low in the water, that large numbers of these fish came on board. The next day, December 18th, a great number of flying-fish were washed on board, and others flew on board in such numbers, that we had, during these two days, enough to serve all hands in abundance. The schooner continued to leak more and more, and we now kept one pump employed almost constantly.

From this time to the 25th, nothing remarkable occurred. Christmas being an idle day, we killed the only remaining pig, all the others, eight in number, having been drowned by the salt water, which almost always flooded the decks when there was a high sea.

On the 27th, saw a sail, standing to the northward; and this day we crossed the equinoctial line, in long. 26° W.; light winds and variable, with dark, rainy weather; thermometer stood at 84° at two p. m. We continued to experience light winds and variable, with dark, rainy weather, for forty-eight hours, when we struck the S. E. trades in lat. 4° S. We had for many days fine breezes from the S. E., and very pleasant weather. I have almost always found this region of the South Atlantic—say from 5° to 20° S. latitude—a delightful part of the ocean to navigate, the weather fine and mild, and the skies very beautiful, with a temperature generally not so hot as to be uncomfortable.

We sailed through these pleasant latitudes without any incident worth remarking until we reached lat. 22° 41' S., on the 6th of January, 1822, when we again had bad, rainy weather, with the wind from the westward. This continued for 24 hours, when we again had a return of the S. E. trades, and pleasant weather.

January 8th,—lat. 24° 20' S. — Last night, the weather being very fine and clear, we saw for the first time what are called the Magellan clouds. They are three in number, and were not far above the horizon. They bore from us about S. S. E., and are evidently clusters of stars; two of them appeared white like the milky-way, the other was dark and indistinctly seen.

January 9th.—At 8 o'clock in the morning, the weather being hazy, with a light breeze from the S. E., the man on the lookout at the mast-head cried out "Land ho!" and told the officer of the deck that he saw something ahead that looked like a small island, and that there were thousands of birds on and around it. In a few minutes every eye was eagerly gazing at the supposed island.

I knew there was no land laid down on any of my charts near where we were, and therefore concluded that it must be the wreck of a ship. As the wind was very light we drew slowly up with the newly discovered object. It soon, however, became visible from the deck, when I took a spy-glass and examined it with close attention, but owing to the constant changes it assumed I was at loss to decide what it was, from its undulating appearance, alternately rising above the water and then again disappearing beneath, until within half a mile's distance, when all doubt was solved, and we found it to be an enormous dead whale floating on its back. It was very much swollen, and at times was apparently some six or eight feet above the water. There were innumerable flocks of wildfowl hovering over and alighting upon it. Many of them appeared to be devouring it, and making loud and wild screams, as if exulting over this grand but accidental feast.

In order to ascertain with more precision its length and size, I hove the schooner to, a short distance to windward, and went in my boat to examine it, which I did to my entire satisfaction.

When approaching near, it became so offensive that I was obliged to keep at a respectful distance to windward, and there watch the numerous flocks of sea-birds that were revelling upon it. In the midst of their din of discordant screams, it was strange to witness with what delight they tore off portions of the fish, and how at each moment their number seemed to augment.

After leaving this scene, I came to the conclusion that dead whales like this are one great cause of so many "dangers" and "small islands," being laid down on all the old charts, which dangers are found not to exist. Such objects as these were probably discovered in dark, windy weather, when it would have been dangerous to have approached near enough to the supposed islands to ascertain what they really were. Thus we have, even at the present time, laid down all over the Atlantic ocean, rocks, shoals, and dangers, the greater part of which do not in reality exist.

January 10th,—lat. 26° 10' S.—During the early part of the last two nights we have seen the four bright stars called the Southern Cross. They are very brilliant, and with a little help of the imagination form a pretty good representation of the Christian cross; and I have no doubt that many of the early Roman Catholic navigators believed they were placed in the heavens to substantiate the truth of the Christian religion.

January 15th.—This day, at noon, we fell in with and boarded the ship *Hannibal,* of Sag Harbor, seven months out on a whaling voyage. They informed me that they had on board 3000 barrels of oil.

At 9 o'clock, p. m., spoke the whaling ship *Fame,* of New London. We were now in lat. 37° 20' S., long. 49° W.

On the 17th January we had clear, pleasant weather, with light and variable winds. At 10 o'clock a. m. our long., by a good lunar observation, was 50° 38' West, lat. at noon 41° 1' South. At 6 o'clock of this day we fell in with the ships *Herald* and *Amazon.* They were cruising in company for whale, and both belonged to Fair Haven, Mass. The captain of the *Herald* came on board to ascertain his longitude; he said they had seen no land for the last two months, and had been too busy to pay much attention to the course or position of the ship; that he knew nothing of lunar observations, and had no chronometer; he was therefore desirous to ascertain the present position of his ship. I had an excellent chronometer on board, and, as the lunar observation taken that day agreed with the chronometer, I told him there was no doubt that I could give him the exact latitude and longitude. He said he had only been eight months at sea, and had then on board 1400 barrels of oil; that the *Amazon* had taken 1100 barrels, and that he should soon steer to the northward on his way home.

When the whale-boat belonging to the *Herald* was alongside the *Sea Serpent,* the boat was higher than the deep-loaded pilot-boat. The captain of the *Herald* said to me:—"Well, captain, you say you are from New York, bound for Lima, but seriously, are you going round Cape Horn in this little whistle-diver?"

"I shall certainly try it, captain," said I, "and hope I shall succeed."

"Well, then, captain," he replied, "but tell me, did you get your life insured before you left home?"

"No," said I, "but I left my family in comfortable circumstances, so that if I should be taken away they will have enough to live upon; besides, I am a good schooner sailor, and am accustomed to these whistle-divers, as you call them."—

"Well, captain," said the whaler, "I must say you have good courage, and I hope you may succeed; but for my part, I had rather kill a hundred whales than go round the Horn in this little craft."

After this dialogue we parted with mutual good wishes for future prosperity and happiness, and each resumed our course upon the great trackless deep. The next day, January 18th, we had strong breezes from the S. E., and though the winds were fresh and strong, and considerable sea, we were able to steer on our S. W. course under reefed sails.

I must not omit to mention the singular fact, of a flock of sea-birds which followed my schooner for the last ten days, namely from lat. 26° S., and were now still hovering near the vessel, sometimes a little ahead, and then again about thirty or forty yards astern. They were generally a little astern and frequently alighted on the water, and appeared to watch every small particle of food or grease that was thrown overboard. They were fifteen in number, and about the size of a common tame pigeon. They are called by seamen, cape pigeons.

From this time to the 22nd of January, nothing remarkable occurred until on that day, when we met with a severe gale from the southward, attended with a high head sea, so that at midnight we were obliged to lay to under a close reefed foresail. We were now in lat. 46° 50' S., long. 58° 26' W. At noon I caught three large albatross, with a hook and line buoyed up by several corks and baited with fat pork. One of the largest measured across his wings, from tip to tip, eight feet four inches. They were covered with white feathers three or four inches thick. They appear to be thus kindly protected by Providence from the cold in these inclement latitudes. In low latitudes, where the weather is hot and sultry, the birds are thinly covered with feathers, which are mostly of high and brilliant colours. The fish also, in hot climates, partake of the same gay and bright colours; such for instance as the parrot fish, the red snapper, and many others. After passing these hot regions and approaching the latitude of

50°, and so on to the latitude of Cape Horn, the birds are generally all white and clothed with an immense mat of down and feathers. Among the fish, likewise, I saw no gay-coloured ones, in these cold regions; on the contrary, I frequently saw large schools of porpoises pied, and sometimes quite white.

While sailing and travelling about the world, I have often been struck with the wisdom and goodness of God, not only to man but to all His creatures, in adapting their condition to the different climates of the earth. We find the coloured man adapted to the sultry, burning climates, and the white man constituted to endure the cold. So it is with beasts, birds, and fish.

I first began to notice the kindness of Providence, when only a boy trading to the islands in the West Indies. I observed that the sheep we used to take there from Connecticut, though thickly covered with wool, would shortly lose their fleeces, and eventually become hairy like goats. On the other hand, the higher the latitude, and where the cold is most intense, the thicker and finer is the fur on the animals, for example, where the bear, seal, and musk ox are found.

As we increased our latitude, the weather became daily more and more rough and boisterous; we encountered storm after storm, and the weather was more cloudy, cold and disagreeable, which kept us reefing and changing almost hourly. On the 26th of January, at 5 a. m., daylight, we made the Falkland Islands, bearing from S. to S. E., distant five leagues; the winds being light and the weather moderate, we stood in shore. The wind being at this time at W. S. W., we were unable to fetch to westward of the islands, and therefore commenced beating up alongshore to weather the westernmost island. These islands appear of a moderate height, and generally rocky and barren. Lat. by obs'. this day 51° 18' S., long. about 61° 6' W. We continued to beat to the westward all this day and the day following; standing off and on the land with open, cloudy weather, and moderate gales from the S. W. Saw a high rock appearing like a lofty sail; marked on the charts Eddystone Rock.

On Monday, January 28th, the land still in sight; at meridian the wind shifted to the N.W., which enabled us to weather the land, and thus we passed to the westward of this group of islands and steered on our course to the southward, and westward towards Cape Horn; lat. by obs. at noon 50° 58' S., long. 61° 50' W. In the afternoon of this day the weather became thick and rainy; passed several tide rips, and saw a number of penguin. The little flock of cape pigeons before alluded to still followed the schooner, our constant companions by day and by night, in sunshine and in tempest. The variation of the compass here is from one and three-quarters to two points easterly. The weather was now cold and disagreeable, temperature by Fahrenheit's therm. 50° above zero.

Tuesday, January 29th.—Light winds and variable. This day the weather appeared to change every hour or two; at times the sun would shine out, and then suddenly disappear and become obscured by a thick fog. This would continue but for a short time, when a strong breeze from the northward would blow all the fog away and the sky remain pretty clear for a few hours, then the sun would again break out and shine for an hour or two, and perhaps another hour would bring a flight of snow. Sometimes, even when the sun was shining, the decks would be covered for a few minutes with snow, which would soon melt away and be followed by a violent shower of rain and hail. In fine, I find it very difficult to describe the weather in this dreary region; though we were in the midst of, summer, we had all the seasons of the year in the course of a day. These continual changes kept us constantly making and taking in sail throughout these twenty-four hours. Lat. by obs. 53° 1' S., long. 64° 0' W.

Jan. 30th.—These twenty-four hours commenced with a strong gale from the westward, with a high head sea running. At 1 p.m., hove to under a two-reefed foresail; dark, cloudy, cold weather, with violent squalls of hail and rain. At midnight the gale moderated, when we again made sail, the schooner labouring violently and making much water. Lat.; by observation, 53° 30' S., long. 64° W.

Jan. 31st. — This day commenced with strong gales from the westward, with a high head sea running; weather dark and gloomy. The wind throughout these twenty-four hours continued to blow strong from the westward, and being directly ahead, we found it impossible to gain to the westward, and were glad to hold our own without losing ground. During the day we had much thunder and lightning. Lat., by observation, 54° 1' S., long. 64° 00' W.

Feb. 1st. — Last night the sky was clear for a little while in the zenith, when we saw the Magellan clouds nearly over our heads. This day we had a continuation of strong gales from the westward, and very bad, stormy weather; we, however, continued to ply to the windward under close-reefed sails, but having a strong westerly gale and a lee current against us, we made but little progress. At 6 a. m. made Staten Land; this land, like the Falklands, appeared cold and dreary, and only a fit habitation for seal and wild fowl, which are here very abundant. The sea in this vicinity also abounds in whales of monstrous bulk. At noon the body of Staten Land bore N. by W., twelve leagues distant. At meridian the sun shone out, when we found our latitude to be 55° 3L' S., long. 64° 8' W.

Feb. 2nd. — This day, like the last, was dark and gloomy, with a continuation of westerly winds, but not so strong as to prevent our plying to windward, under close-reefed sails. The thermometer fell down to 45° above zero. In consequence of contrary winds and a lee current we gained but little on our course during these twenty-four hours. Lat., by observation, 56° 20' S., long. 65° 27' W.

Feb. 3rd. — On this day, when within about fifty miles of Cape Horn, a terrible gale commenced blowing from the westward. It continued to increase until it blew a perfect hurricane, and soon created a mountainous sea. We got our foreyard on deck, and hove the schooner to, under the head of a new foresail. I then ordered all the bulwarks and waist-boards to be knocked away, that nothing might impede the water from passing over the

SCHOONER *SEA-SERPENT*

134

decks without obstruction, otherwise so great a quantity would have lodged in the lee-waist that our little schooner would have been water-logged and swamped with the weight of it. With crowbars and axes the waist-boards were all demolished, and the sea broke over the decks and passed off without injury to our little *barque*, and she rose like a stormy petrel on the top of the sea, which threatened every moment to swallow us in its abyss.

The ocean was lashed into a white foam by the fury of the tempest. The same weather continued with but little intermission for a space of five days. During a great part of this time it was almost impossible to look to windward, so violent were the hail and snow squalls. In the midst of this tempest, my officers and men behaved nobly: the most perfect order prevailed; not a whisper of fear or contention was heard during the whole of our perilous situation. To render the men more comfortable, I removed them all from the forecastle to the cabin, where they continued to live until we had fairly doubled the Cape and found better weather.

My Italian passenger was terribly alarmed during the tempest, and entreated me, in piteous tones, to put away for Rio Janeiro. He said if I would do so, he would instantly sign an agreement to give me all his interest in the vessel and cargo. I resolutely declined his offer, and told him that while we had masts and sails, and the vessel would float under us, I would never put back.

This Cape is rendered more dreadful from the fact of its inhospitable position, and being so far removed from any civilized port. It is a cold, cheerless, barbarous coast, where no provision, or supplies of any kind, can be had in case of shipwreck or disaster, so that the greatest vigilance and perseverance are necessary to bear the many obstacles, that present themselves.

Feb. 8th. — The gale abated, and we were again enabled to make sail and ply to the westward. Our faithful little pigeons had hovered about us during the long tempest, and now resumed the journey with us. We got an observation of the sun this day at noon, and found ourselves in lat. 57° 33' S., long. 66° 12' W.

Feb. 9th. — We had, throughout these twenty-four hours, favourable gales from the N. E., and open, cloudy weather. Made all sail and steered to the westward, and gained 160 miles distance on a direct course, and everything began to wear a better appearance. We made better progress this day than we had done since our arrival in these high southern latitudes. Lat., by observation at noon, 57° 16' S., long, by chronometer 71° 4' W.

Feb. 10th.—This day commenced with strong gales from the southward, with dark, squally weather; under reefed sails standing to the northward and westward, made a distance of 155 miles per log. Towards noon the sun shone out, when we found ourselves, at meridian, in lat. 55° 44' S., long. 74° 48 W. We had now fairly doubled Cape Horn; and I hoped in a few days to descend to lower latitudes, and find warmer and better weather. It was now fifteen days since we made the Falkland Islands, so that we were from thirteen to fifteen days weathering Cape Horn, which is not an unusual length of time, and had our vessel been a good ship of three or four hundred tons, we should have suffered nothing in comparison with what we did undergo, in a deep loaded, pilot-boat schooner, of one hundred and forty tons, leaking badly. From the 10th of February to the 16th, we generally had light and variable winds from the northward and westward, so that we made but slow progress during the week, and nothing worth recording occurred.

Feb. 17th.—This day commenced with light breezes from the S. W., and fine weather. During the night, in a squall, a small fish was washed on board. It weighed before it was dressed about half a pound, and in appearance was not unlike a brook trout, except that it had a greenish colour. I directed the cook to prepare it for my breakfast, and told him to fry it with a few slices of salt pork. At breakfast, I divided the fish between my passenger, the chief mate and myself. We all ate the fish with a good relish, and returned on deck; but very soon after, we were all taken sick: the mate was seized with violent vomiting, and became death-like pale and languid.— The passenger was also sick, but not so much so as the mate. I was not very ill, but felt a burning sensation in my mouth and throat for several hours afterwards. Upon examining the scales and intestines of the fish, and the knife with which it was cleaned, we found them all of a deep greenish colour, indicating that the fish must have been very poisonous. What it was I know not. It is remarkable that one of so small a size could poison three persons.

During the remainder of this day we had light breezes from the W. and fine weather. We only made about 100 miles on our course through these twenty-four hours; at noon our lat. by obs. was 47° 56' S., long. 78° 17' W.

From the 17th of February, to the 22nd of the same month, we had light winds from the southward and westward, and generally good weather; we steered to the northward. We were daily getting the weather more mild and pleasant, as we approached the lower latitudes. We met with nothing worth remarking during the last five days. We were now in. lat. 38° 45' S., long. 79° 29' W.

Feb. 23rd.—We had fresh breezes from the S. W. and fine weather throughout these twenty-four hours, and made 166 miles distance to the northward. Lat. by obs. at noon 36° 0' S., long, per chron. 79° 34' West.

Feb. 24th.—This day commenced with fine fresh breezes from the southward, and very pleasant weather, which we sensibly enjoyed after getting through those tempestuous regions into the bright and gentle Pacific Ocean, which daily became more and more mild and tranquil. At 8 o'clock in the morning we made the island of Massafuero bearing N. N. W., about eight leagues distant. At 11 o'clock a. m. it bore west, three leagues distant. This island lies in lat. 33° 45' S:, long. 80° 38' W. It is a high, abrupt, rugged looking place about fifteen or twenty miles long and perhaps five or six broad. The shores are very steep, and I believe it is only accessible on the N. W. side in a little bay, where boats can land in good weather. It has no harbour, notwithstanding it was formerly a famous island for taking seal. Some twenty-five or thirty years ago, several good voyages were made by ships from New England, which took seal skins from this island to Canton in China, where they disposed of them, and returned to the United States, richly laden with teas and other China goods. One of these voyages was made by a ship called the *Neptune,* commanded by Captain Daniel T. Green (in which were two young men belonging to my native town, from whom I obtained this information). This ship was owned in New Haven, Connecticut, and took from this island fifty thousand seal skins and sold them in Canton for $2 each, and thence returned to New York in the year 1799, with a cargo of teas, silk goods, *nankeens,* &c.. The owners and crew cleared by the voyage about $100,000.

This trade was carried on for several years very advantageously, until at length all the seal were killed or driven away from the island. The sealing ships were then compelled to search for a new field, in distant seas and on lonely desert islands, where the seal had never been disturbed by man. When they first commenced killing seal at Massafuero, the animals were so tame and gentle that thousands were killed with clubs. These poor animals, unconscious of the danger, made no attempt to escape; but in a few years after they became so knowing and shy, that it was difficult to kill them, except by stratagem. I have subsequently seen them in different places along the coast of Peru, and found them so extremely wild and timid that they would plunge into the water when approached, and at this time it is very difficult to kill them, even with spears and muskets.

This day we also saw and passed by Juan Fernandez. This island is not so high as Massafuero, but is more fertile and productive. It lies in latitude 33° 46' S., longitude 79° 6' W. It belongs to Chile, and is about 400 miles west of Valparaiso. It has a tolerable harbour on the south side, and has been used lately by the Chilean Government as a sort of Botany Bay for state prisoners. It has become a place of general interest to the world from its having been made the locality of Robinson Crusoe's adventures, by De Foe.

It was now one hundred days since we left New York, and we had still more than 1000 miles to sail before we could reach Lima, but as we expected to get into the S. E. trade winds in a day or two from this time, I anticipated the remainder of the passage with pleasure.

February 25th.—Throughout these twenty-four hours, we had fine breezes from the southward, and very pleasant weather. We were now sailing with a fair wind, with all our light sails set. Our little schooner was well adapted to these smooth seas and gentle breezes; we made 190 miles during the last twenty-four hours, and were at noon in latitude 30° 23' S., longitude 80° 28' W.

February 26th.—Fresh breezes from the S. E., and clear, pleasant weather throughout these twenty-four hours. We had now taken the regular S. E. trades. It was delightful to sail before the wind in this mild climate and smooth sea (which is so appropriately called the Pacific Ocean), after having been buffeted and tossed about off Cape Horn so long in so small a vessel. During the last twenty-four hours our little vessel made 200 miles with perfect ease, and almost without shifting a single sail. Lat. by obs. at noon 27° 4' S., long. 80° 28' W.

From the 26th of February to the 5th of March, we had a continuation of the S. E. trade winds, and fine pleasant weather, running constantly on our direct course, and daily making from 150 to 200 miles.

Our friendly birds, which had constantly followed us for the last fifty-six days, from the coast of Brazil and round Cape Horn, still kept about us. They were not so constantly near our vessel as before we came down into these mild latitudes, but they made little excursions and then returned. I sometimes missed them for an hour or two, and feared, in two or three instances, that they had entirely left us and would no more return to cheer us, but to my agreeable surprise they always came, and were at this time within a few yards of our stern, and appeared attached to our little *barque* and to the hands that occasionally fed them. They were indeed a great source of entertainment, and their fidelity was a constant theme of conversation and interest to us.

March 5th, 1822.—This day commenced with light winds from the S. E., and, as usual, fine, clear weather. At 4 o'clock in the afternoon we made the island of Lorenzo, bearing about N. B., twenty-five miles distant. At 8 in the evening we got near the island. It being too late to run into port, I concluded to stand off and on under its lee and wait until daylight to run in and anchor.

March 6th.—We came to anchor near the forts at Callao—the seaport of Lima—all well, after a passage of 110 days from New York.

It was not until we came to anchor that our little guardian birds left us and flew out of the harbour.

We found Callao and Lima in the hands of the patriots (as the natives of the country were called), and that the Spanish army had retreated to the interior; of course, the blockade was raised, and the object of my voyage in a great measure defeated.

I have before stated, that we purchased this little, fast-sailing vessel, in order to evade the blockade by superior sailing, otherwise it would have been more advantageous to the owners to have bought a more burthensome vessel at a less cost, and far more comfortable for me to perform a voyage round Cape Horn in such an one, than it was in a small pilot-boat schooner.

After entering my vessel and going through the necessary forms at Callao, I forthwith proceeded up to Lima, and presented my letters of introduction to several gentlemen, who were merchants residing in that city, and was not long in making an arrangement with Don Francisco X. Iscue, a respectable merchant, to take charge of my business, and act as my general agent and consignee. Señor Iscue was a native of Old Spain, but was married to a lady born in Lima. He had an interesting family, and was an honest, worthy man, and a very correct merchant. Through this gentleman I disposed of most of that part of my cargo which was at all adapted to the market, such as provisions, and a part of my manufactured goods. All the butter sold at $1 per lb. Flour was at this time selling at $30 per barrel. Some articles of my cargo sold at an enormous profit, while many others would not bring prime cost.

Soon after my arrival at Callao, the ship *America,* Captain De Koven, of New York, arrived with a full cargo of flour. I believe he brought about 3500 barrels, which were sold at a very great profit. To Captain De Koven I sold my quicksilver at invoice price, which amounted to about $3500.

As all communication was cut off between Lima and the interior, I was unable to dispose of the quicksilver at any price, except to Captain De Koven. He was bound to Canton, and took the article at invoice price to dispose of it in China. I subsequently lent him $11,500 in dollars (which, together with the quicksilver, amounted to $15,000). and took his bill on the owners of the *America,* in New York, for the amount at sixty days sight. The owners of the ship were Messrs. Hoyt and Tom, Elisha Tibbets, and Stephen Whitney.

I soon had all my cargo transported to Lima, and in about twenty days after my arrival sold the schooner *Sea Serpent,* for ten thousand five hundred dollars. Such goods as I could not dispose of at private sale, I sold at public auction; and on the 6th of June, 1822, closed the accounts of the voyage, and I am sorry to add, made little or nothing for my owners. My own private adventure sold tolerably well; and what, with my wages, commissions, etc., I made for myself what is called a saving voyage.

I waited about a fortnight for a passage to Panama, but was unable to obtain one. On the 10th of June, I was offered the command of the fine Baltimore-built brig *Dick* burthen 207 tons, and only two years old. This vessel belonged to the Italian gentleman who came out as a passenger with me in the *Sea Serpent.* He was desirous of employing the *Dick* in the coasting trade, on the western coast of Chile and Peru. I was also glad of employment for a few months, until the sickly season had passed away in Panama and Chagrés, (having decided to return to the United States by the way of Panama and across the Isthmus of

Darien to Chagrés.) The Italian was an honest man, but, not having been bred a merchant, relied on me to manage the voyage of his brig.

After I had disposed of the *Sea Serpent,* I paid off the mates and seamen, and allowed each of them two months' extra pay, according to law, and then procured nearly all of them situations on board of other vessels. Both mates, when I left Callao, were pleasantly situated as officers, on board of English vessels, coasting between Chile and Peril; and the seamen got good berths and generous wages; so that none of my crew were left in distress, or unprovided with employment.

As Mr. B. the owner of the brig had decided to proceed with her down the coast of Peru, to Truxillo and Pagusmayo, and there purchase a cargo of sugar, rice, and such other articles of provision as were then much wanted in Lima, I lost no time in shipping officers and seamen, and getting ready for the voyage, which under ordinary circumstances would require about two months to perform. On the 28th of July we were ready for sea.

Callao is the seaport of Lima, and lies in lat. 12° 2' S., long. 77° 4' W., seven or eight miles west of Lima. Callao is strongly protected by forts, castles and walls, with broad and wide exterior ditches. To a stranger the castles at first view appear like a small walled city. Outside of these vast and expensive fortifications, there is a considerable number of houses, magazines and shops, generally lying along the bay, and in some places extending back, perhaps, a short quarter of a mile.

This village is called Callao, and the fortifications are called the Castles of Callao. The road between Lima and the port is level and good. The port of Callao is formed by a bay which is sheltered by its own points and the island of St. Lorenzo, which lies at the south entrance, about eight or ten miles distant from the Castles at Callao. As I have no map or book before me, and write entirely from memory, I may perhaps make some little error in the distance, but not in the main facts. Callao Bay is a fine, broad, clear expanse of water, and deep enough for a line-of-battle ship in almost any part of it, and on the whole, I should pronounce it a very safe and good harbour, particularly in this mild and gentle climate, where there are no violent gales or tempests. In this respect the inhabitants of this coast are favoured beyond any part of the world I have ever visited. The oldest men in this country know nothing of a storm or a violent gale of wind; so uniform is the weather, that the Fahr. thermometer in Lima rarely varies more than six or eight degrees. It generally ranges between 75° and 80°. Although it is sometimes hot at noonday, the nights are cool and comfortable, owing to the snow and ice in the mountains not very far distant in the interior.

When Peru was a colony of Spain, Lima was a populous and comparatively rich city; but in consequence of continued wars and revolutions it has become poor. For the last eight years there had been a constant demand for young men to join the armies, which has rendered the population less than it was previously. The city of Lima, the capital of Peru, lies about seven miles from the sea, and is pleasantly situated at the foot of the Cordilleras. The little river Rimac takes its rise in the mountains and runs through the city, and supplies the inhabitants with an abundance of excellent water. Over this stream there is a fine stone bridge with six arches. On this bridge and in recesses are placed seats for the citizens, which renders it a favourite resort for the elite of the city. It is said that before the revolution, Lima contained about eighty thousand inhabitants; at the time of which I write it numbers only about sixty thousand, exclusive of the military, who I should judge were about eight or ten thousand. There are several large churches and public buildings, which have rather an imposing appearance.

The cathedral in the centre of the city, which forms the east side of the Plaza Maza, is the grand resort of all the better classes of people, and is a pleasant place. In consequence of the earthquakes to which Lima is subject, the houses are generally built low, not often more than one or two stories high, and of very slight materials, namely, dried clay and reeds, with a light coat of plaster, and then whitewashed or painted. I believe that if it should blow and rain a few hours as it does sometimes in the

Bay of Honduras, that the whole city would be washed away; but fortunately for the inhabitants, it never rains in the city. The high and long chain of Cordilleras in the interior, acts as a perfect conductor for the clouds and storms. There only the clouds break and the rain falls in torrents. It therefore becomes necessary, notwithstanding the heavy dews, to irrigate the fields and gardens in the neighbourhood of Lima.

I think the city is about two miles long, and one and a half broad. Through the principal streets water is conducted from the Rimac. This tends very much to cool and cleanse the town, which, if blessed with peace and a good government, would be a very delightful city, bating an occasional alarm of earthquakes.

A few weeks before my arrival, the Castles at Callao and the city of Lima, were vacated by the Spanish army and taken possession of by General St. Martin and Lord Cochran; the former at the head of 8,000 or 10,000 Chilean and Peruvian troops, and the latter, the admiral, commanding the Chilean squadron of two or three frigates and several smaller vessels. I believe there was very little fighting, but a kind of capitulation was agreed upon between the parties. The Spanish army marched out and retreated into the interior, when the patriot army took possession with little or no bloodshed. Still the inhabitants of Lima were, during the time I remained there, in constant dread of a return of the Spanish army. The city and its dependencies were daily agitated and unsettled, and the whole country was convulsed with war. The Government was almost daily making forced loans and contributions upon the inhabitants, which caused them to secrete their money for fear of its being taken from them. Every fine horse belonging to private individuals was seized for the use of the army; even the horses of foreigners were sometimes taken, but they were generally returned after a suitable remonstrance to the commanding officer.

This has been rather a long digression, and I will again return to my narrative.

The brig *Dick,* under my command, was ready for sea on the 28th of July. Before sailing, I wrote the particulars of the voyage to my owners, and also to my family up to this date, and the next day sailed for Truxillo, with the owner of the brig on board.

It was 6 o'clock in the evening when we got under way; we had light winds from the S. E., and foggy weather during the night, and ran to the leeward under easy sail until daylight.

July 30th.—During the first and middle part of these twenty-four hours we had a continuation of light winds and thick weather. After running about fifty-six miles log distance, it lighted up, when we found ourselves in mid channel between the islands of Mazorque and Pelada, which are about two leagues asunder.

No observation of the sun, it being obscured by fog.

31st.—First and middle part of twenty-four hours light breezes from the S. E. with a continuation of cloudy weather. At 11 o'clock in the forenoon, we passed a schooner beating up the coast. We set our ensign, and indicated our wish to speak him, but the unsocial fellow would not shorten sail, and appeared to avoid us. At noon saw a ship running down to the westward. We continued to run along shore to the northward, and made about 100 miles by the log. At noon our lat. by obs. was 10° 29' S., long, about 77° 50' W.

Aug. 1st.—At 1 o'clock in the afternoon we saw the land, bearing E. S. E. eight or ten leagues distant. We had light breezes and calm weather all the twenty-four hours, and only made ninety-six miles, running down along the land, generally at a distance of ten leagues. Lat. by obs. at noon 9° 14' S.

Aug. 2nd.—First and middle part of these twenty-four hours, light airs from the S. E. and clear, pleasant weather. At 12 midnight, hove to and lay by until 3 a. m., daylight, when we made sail. At five in the morning, saw the island of Guanap, bearing S. E. about four miles distant. We then hauled in shore. Brisk breezes at S. E. and fine, clear, pleasant weather. At 10 o'clock in the forenoon, the city of Truxillo bore east, and in half an hour afterwards we came to anchor at Guanchaco, in seven fathoms water; the church at that place bearing E. by N. about a league distant. This is an Indian village situated on the beach of the sea, and is the seaport of Truxillo. It lies in lat. 8° 8' S., and long, about 79° 0' west of London,

I should perhaps rather have called Guanchaco the roadstead or anchoring ground of Truxillo, for it certainly cannot properly be called a harbour. It is open to the broad ocean, and has nothing to shelter ships that touch or trade on this part of the coast. The Indians who live in the village of Guanchaco are expert boatmen, and with their own boats transport all the goods and merchandise landed at that port for Truxillo, or exported therefrom. They are perhaps 500 to 800 in number, are governed by their own *alcalde* and under officers, and live almost entirely by boating and fishing. The ships that touch here cannot with any safety use their own boats, and always employ the boats or canoes of the Indians, the surf being too high to venture off and on without the aid of these men, who are almost amphibious. They are trained to swimming from their infancy, and commence with a small *balsa*, in the surf within the reefs, and by degrees, as they grow older and larger, venture through the surf, and out upon the broad ocean.

These *balsas*, are made of reeds bound firmly together, with a hole near the after end, for one person; the forward end is tapered, and turned up like a skate or a Turkish shoe. Those for children are perhaps from five to eight feet long, and those used by the men are generally about ten or twelve feet long, and about as large in circumference as a small sized barrel. An Indian placed in one of these *balsas* with a paddle bids defiance to the roaring billows and breaking surf. I have seen the men go off through it in one of these reedy boats, when it seemed impossible that a human being could live in the surf, and have with great anxiety observed them at times when a high rolling sea threatened to overwhelm them, watch the approaching roller and duck their heads down close to the reed boat, and let the billow pass over them, like a seal or a wild duck, and force their way with perfect confidence through the surf, where no white man would for a moment dare to venture.

One of these men would, for half a dollar, convey a letter from the shore through the surf, to a ship laying at anchor in the roads, when no boat dare attempt it. I was told that for a small sum of money, one of these Indians would take a valuable piece of silk goods (secured in oiled cloth and fastened round his body) on shore, and deliver it to the owner perfectly dry, even in a dark night. The moment they land they take up the *balsa* and place it in an upright position in the sun to drain and dry, and thus it is kept ready at a moment's warning for any employment that may offer.

While here, I used sometimes to amuse myself with throwing small pieces of copper coin into the water, to see the Indian boys dive to the bottom and pick them up. I never could learn that any of these, Indians were drowned, though the people of Trux-illo told us of many accidents, when white men were drowned, in attempting to land in a high surf.

The morning we arrived at Guanchaco, there came in also an English ship from Lima, and anchored near our brig.—Very soon after, a large launch, manned with nine Indians, came alongside of us, to take the captains, supercargoes, and passengers of both vessels on shore. As there was considerable surf on, great anxiety was expressed by the supercargoes and passengers, respecting the safety of landing. I had a conversation with the *patroon* of the boat, on the subject of landing. He said that if we would commit ourselves entirely into his hands, there was no danger; and that he supposed the gentlemen would be willing to pay half a dollar each, if landed dry and in perfect safety. This we all readily agreed to, and soon started for the shore. I think we were five in number; and as we approached the shore, a few yards outside the surf, the sea was terrific, and breaking "feather white."

Some of the gentlemen were in favour of returning, but were soon overruled by the majority. I attentively watched the eye of the *patroon*, who appeared cool and collected, and, by his manner, inspired me with confidence in his ability to perform what he had undertaken. He requested the gentlemen who feared the result, not to survey the scene, but to lie down in the stern-sheets of the boat, and thus give him room to manage the boat according to his own judgement. At this moment, I saw a man on the beach, on the watch for a favourable instant for us to pull for the shore. The man on the shore and our *patroon* made signals with a handkerchief on a cane. The boat's head was kept off shore until the signal was given and answered, to dash through the surf. In an instant the boat was wheeled round with her head towards the land, when every man pulled to the utmost of his strength, and in a few minutes we were safe within the breakers. These strong, brave fellows, then took each a passenger on his back, and carried him ashore in great triumph. We were all so sensibly touched with the conduct of these men, that many dollars were voluntarily thrown into their hats and caps; and a thrill of gratitude passed over my mind, that will remain with me till the hour of my death. We call these people savages, and say that they are incapable of great actions. I defy the white man to contend with them in the management of a boat in the surf, on the seashore.

The *alcalde* furnished us with horses, and we were soon on the road to the city of Truxillo, which is pleasantly situated on level ground, about eight or ten miles from the landing at Guanchaco. I think it contained, at this time, about eight or ten thousand inhabitants. There are two or three considerable churches; many of the houses arc well built, and have a comfortable appearance.

The ground and gardens around the city are well cultivated, and produce abundance of excellent fruit; and the whole aspect of the town and its vicinity is extremely pleasant. Although this place is located so near the equator, the climate is not uncomfortably warm. There is, however, a great drawback to a residence in this place, in the frequency of earthquakes. I was told by some of the most respectable citizens of Truxillo, that the town had been two or three times nearly destroyed by earthquakes, and that the great earthquakes were generally periodical,—say at intervals of forty years—that some thirty years had now passed away without a very destructive one, and that they had serious fears that they should experience another terrible convulsion before many years should elapse.

We found here no sugars or other produce to purchase, nor could we hear of any of consequence in the neighbouring towns to leeward. Two vessels from Lima had lately been here, and to the adjacent towns, and bought up all the inhabitants had to dispose of.

After remaining here a few days, my owner and myself returned to Guanchaco, without making any purchases, except some poultry and fruit for sea-stores.

On our way back to the landing, we passed over very extensive ruins, which appeared at least two miles in length: they were the remains of clay walls, and various fragments of what had once been an extensive city of the Incas. We saw also a large mound near Guanchaco. It was 50 to 80 feet high, and, perhaps, from 150 to 200 feet long. These mounds were no doubt made by, the ancient Peruvians, and are found all along this coast. Some of them are very high and large, others quite small. I have seen a great variety of Indian relics, that were dug out from this mound, such as earthen drinking vessels, made to resemble cats, dogs, monkeys, and other animals; others, again, were made exactly to resemble a fish, with a handle on its back, and its mouth open to drink from. These articles were well executed, and of very fine clay. The present race of Peruvians are altogether incapable of manufacturing anything of the kind equal to these ancient Indian relics. I have no doubt, if these mounds were fairly excavated, that a great variety of valuable Indian relics could be found, which are now hidden from the world.

We arrived at the landing on Thursday, August 8th, in the afternoon, and found too much surf on the beach to attempt going on board until the next morning, and as there was no hotel or tavern in Guanchaco, we took up our abode for the night with the *alcalde* or chief magistrate of the village. This person was an intelligent Indian, who had in his early life made several voyages to Manilla, and appeared familiar with all parts of the western coast of Peru. He seemed to be a sensible, judicious person, and managed and governed the people of Guanchaco in a quiet, paternal manner. During the evening he entertained us with a narration of his voyages from Peru to the Philippine Islands, when Peru was a colony of Spain. He also related to us many anecdotes of his race, the ancient and rightful owners of this bloodstained soil.

The high mounds all along this part of the coast appear to be monuments of their wrongs and sufferings, and call to mind the days when Pizarro, with his band of merciless adventurers, sacrificed thousands and tens of thousands of these innocent worshippers of the sun, robbed them of their gold, and finally despoiled them of home and country. Even to the present day, these poor people are not exempt from severe persecutions in the way of taxation and oppression. They are now forcibly taken from their quiet homes to fill the ranks led by military chiefs, and thus compelled to mingle in the deadly strife of contending parties. Whether the one or the other governs, it is to them only a change of masters, for they cannot be supposed to feel any interest for, or sympathy with, either of them. And thus it has ever been in this wicked and unjust world, the strong triumph over and oppress the weak.

The good *alcalde* had supper prepared for us, and placed mattresses and blankets on the tables for Mr. B. and myself. Previous to retiring to rest I took a stroll round the house, and saw, beneath a shed or back *piazza*, three of the *alcalde's* children, little boys, I should judge between ten years old and three, lying asleep on a raw dry bullock's hide, covered only with another. The air was chilly, and it struck me at the moment as inhuman treatment to expose children thus to the open air without other covering than a raw hide. I immediately inquired of our friendly host why he thus exposed his children. His answer was, that it was their general custom to harden them and give them good constitutions; that he himself was brought up in the same manner; and being thus inured to the cold while young, they felt no inconvenience from it in after life.

In the morning the sea was smooth, and the surf not bad. After taking leave of the polite and friendly *alcalde*, we left Guanchaco in the Indian launch, got safe on board, and at 3 o'clock on the 9th of August, weighed anchor and made sail for Payta.

After getting our anchor on board, we found the stock broken in two pieces, and thus rendered unfit for use. We steered to the westward along shore with a good S. E. trade wind, and pleasant weather. Through the night we had moderate breezes and a continuation of fine weather. At 5 o'clock in the morning, daylight, saw the islands of Lobos de Mer and Lobos de Terra, bearing S. W., three leagues distant. They are of moderate height, and without trees or cultivation. Towards noon the winds became light, inclining to a calm. Lat. by obs. 6° 32' S., long, about 81° W.

On the 10th of August, we had light winds and fine weather, and made but little progress on our course during the day, still steering down along shore with the land in sight.

Aug. 11th.—This day, like the last, commenced with light airs and calm, warm weather. At 8 p. m., Point de Ajuga bore E., two leagues distant. During the night, light airs and fine weather. At daylight, saw Point de Payta, bearing N. E., eight leagues distant; at 8, got near the Point, and steered up the Bay of Payta. At 11, a breeze sprung up from the S. E., when we ran up the bay and came to anchor at noon, in nine fathoms water, directly opposite the town. We had little or no cargo to dispose of, and there was no freight to be obtained, consequently we remained here only twenty-four hours, and got ready for sea.

Payta is situated on a fine bay of the same name, and is the principal seaport of Puira, a very considerable town in the interior, some ten or fifteen leagues distant from this place.

The town of Payta is located very near the beach, and the whole surrounding country for some miles distant is a barren, sandy desert, not even affording fresh water. The inhabitants are supplied with this article, brought from a little river running into the head of the bay, at a distance of six or eight miles. The town probably contains about 1,500 to 2,000 inhabitants of all colours; a great portion, however, are Indians, and a mixture of the Spanish and Indian races.

The houses are generally built of cane and straw, with thatched roofs. It is a very healthy place, and the people, who are generally poor, live to a great age. It lies in lat. 5° 3' S., long. 81° W. of London, and is one of the best harbours on the western coast of Peru. It is a great resort for American and English whale ships. The bay of Payta is large and clean, and I believe the whalers send their boats to the little river at its head, and soon get a bountiful supply of pure, wholesome water; at the same time the ships are safe and quiet while they remain in this capacious bay.

At 2 o'clock in the afternoon of the 12th, with a fine fresh S. E. trade wind, we sailed out of this bay, bound for Guayaquil. At 6 p. m., got abreast of Point de Parina, about a league off shore; at the same time saw Cape Blanco bearing N., half E., twenty-four miles distant. During the night we had fresh breezes, with a little rain. At 6 a. m. saw the land, bearing from S.W. to N. E., five or six leagues distant. Lat. by obs. at noon, 3° 37' S. At this time Point Los Picos bore S. E., distant about four leagues.

Aug. 13th.—This day commenced with light airs from the S., with very warm weather. At 4 p. m., passed near the American whale-ship *Rosalie,* of Warren, R. I., which was lying at anchor, near Tumbes. This ship had been thirteen months absent from the United States, and had only taken 200 barrels of oil.

At 8 p.m., we came to anchor in five fathoms' water, near the mouth of the Tumbes river, the small island of Santa Clara bearing N. by W., distant about four leagues. Light wind at N. E. Here we lay at anchor all night.

Aug. 14th.—This day commenced with light breezes from the N. E., and fine weather. At 8 a. m., got under way with a light wind from the N. W. by N. The tide now commenced making up the river, which enabled us to gain ground, beating up with its assistance until noon, when the wind became more favourable, from the W. S. W. At 3 p. m., got abreast of the west end of the island of Puna; pleasant breezes and fine weather.

At 7 p. m., we came to anchor in four and a half fathoms of

water, the east end of Puna then bearing N. N. W., four leagues distant. It being dark, and having no pilot on board, I judged it imprudent to make sail, and therefore remained at anchor during the night.

Aug. 15th.—This day commenced with clear, pleasant weather, with light winds and variable. At 6 a. m., received a pilot on board, and at eight got under way with the flood tide and stood up the river, which had now become more narrow, but was still deep and not difficult to ascend. The banks along the river on both sides are low, but the land rises as you recede from the river into the interior to immense mountains, many of which are volcanic. We continued to beat up the stream, and at 6 p. m., just before dark, came to anchor in the river opposite the city of Guayaquil in six fathoms of water, a short quarter of a mile off the town.

It is about forty miles from Guayaquil to the island of Puna, where the river pilots reside, and it is at this place that the river fairly commences; for below Puna, it may more properly be called a wide bay or gulf opening into the sea.

We found lying at Guayaquil some fifteen or twenty sail of vessels of different nations, four or five of which were American ships and brigs, among them the ship *Canton,* of New York, and the brig *Canton,* of Boston. The names of the others I do not now recollect.

After lying here a few days, undecided what to do with, or how to employ, the brig, my owner, on the 22nd of August, sold his vessel for $14,000, to John O'Sullivan, Esq., captain and supercargo of the ship *Canton.* Captain O'Sullivan gave the command of the brig to Lieutenant Hudson, now Captain Hudson, of the U. S. Navy.

He loaded her in this port for a voyage to Upper Peru. At this time there were lying at Guayaquil two large Calcutta ships loaded with Indian goods. From these ships Captain O'Sullivan, purchased the greater-part of a cargo for the *Dick.* The balance was made up of cocoa, and a few other articles. Myself, officers and crew were now paid off, and left the vessel in charge of the new owners.

I was anxious to return home to New York, and of course did not regret being sold out of employment. I had long been acquainted with Captain O'Sullivan, and was glad to meet him here. I also met with another acquaintance in the person of Francis Coffin, Esq., supercargo of the brig *Canton*.

Mr. Coffin got a fine freight of cocoa for Cadiz. I think it amounted to $17,500. I was glad to have good fortune attend him, as he was and is, if alive, an honourable gentlemanly man, of sterling worth and high integrity.

I was now living on shore, anxiously waiting a passage for Panama, to return home across the isthmus. Captain O'Sullivan had with him three or four young gentlemen, belonging to New York. These young men joined the ship *Canton,* in New York, as ordinary seamen, but not liking a sea-life were anxious to return home. Captain O'Sullivan gave two of them liberty to leave the ship, but would not supply them with money. He told me, however, that if I thought proper to take them along with me, that he had no doubt their friends in New York would refund the money I should expend in paying their passages back to the U. S.; and as they were here destitute, I consented to take them, pay their passages and other necessary expenses to New York, and rely upon the honour of their families to refund me the amount when we should arrive there.

After waiting a few days, we heard of a small coasting vessel which was to leave this place for Panama in a few days. She was a full-rigged brig, of about twenty-five tons burthen, with a cap-tain, boatswain, and eight men before the mast. A vessel of the same size in the U. S. would have been sloop-rigged, and pro-vided with a captain, one man, and a boy. In this vessel I agreed for a passage to Panama for myself and my two young American friends. This brig was called *Los dos Hermanos.* There were two other (Guayaquil gentlemen) passengers, besides myself and the before-named young men, who agreed to sleep on deck; as I paid one hundred dollars for my passage, I was supplied with a berth in the cabin, if it deserved the name, for in fact it was more like a dog's kennel than a cabin. It had no windows or sky-light, and was nearly filled with bags and boxes, and had only two berths, and no table. The two passengers belonging to Guayaquil, occupied one of the berths, and I the other.

Guayaquil lies in lat. 2° 12' S., long. 79° 42 W., and is about 150 miles to the southward of Quito. The city of Guayaquil lies on the right bank of the river, and contains about 20,000 inhabitants, and although built of wood, a great portion of the houses are large and comfortable, and well adapted to the climate. Several of the public buildings are spacious and firmly built with tiled roofs, among which are the customhouse, college, and hospital. The city is located on low, level ground, and of course difficult to drain, which at certain seasons of the year renders it very unhealthy. The educated classes of society are polite and hospitable. The ladies dress in good taste, and are decidedly the handsomest women on the western coast of this continent; in fact, the beauty of the Guayaquil ladies is proverbial. The lower classes are a desperate looking race. They are a mixture of the Spaniard, Indian, and Negro, and appear ripe for any kind of villainy or disorder.

The principal wealth of Guayaquil proceeds from the cultivation of cocoa, which is their staple article. They also export timber, boards, hides, and some tobacco. The cocoa plantations lie on both sides of the river for several miles above the city. It is brought to Guayaquil upon floating rafts of light buoyant wood called, in this country, *balzas*. These rafts are in general use for all kinds of transportation. Many of the poorer classes live upon them. They float up and down the river with perfect ease and safety. In them the cocoa is taken on board of the ships that load here. On these *balzas* they erect tents and awnings, and thus protect themselves and their cargoes from the sun and rain. Along the river and thence down to the sea-coast, the land is very flat, and in the rainy seasons a great portion of the low grounds are inundated; consequently the inhabitants in such places build their houses on large timbers, or posts, some eight or ten feet above the ground, and find it necessary to have ladders to get into them. When flooded in the rainy seasons, they pass from house to house in boats.

In this warm latitude, where the sun is nearly vertical, the weather is generally very hot, and the vegetation extremely luxuriant and rank; consequently none but those born and reared in this climate can reside in these low lands on the banks of the rivers and creeks, with any degree of safety.

To the eastward, some ten or fifteen leagues in the interior, I, beheld lofty mountains rising one above another, until at last the eye rested on the majestic Chimborazo. There it stands, a mountain on the top of other mountains, terminating in a lofty sugar-loaf, snow-capped peak, alone, in its own grand and unrivalled sublimity; and although some seventy-five or eighty miles from Guayaquil, it appears as though it were within a very short distance. This grand sight, however, is not an everyday occurrence. On the contrary, one may remain at Guayaquil for several days, and even weeks, without getting a good view of the peak. When the clouds are dispelled, you behold the whole mountain from the base to the top in all its beauty and grandeur. The sight of this sublime object richly rewards the traveller for the expense and privation of coming to this country.

While I remained here the weather was extremely warm, and one can easily imagine that to be supplied with ice and ice-cream must have been a most acceptable luxury, and so we found it. As often as once or twice a week I saw a flag hoisted at a favourite café as a signal for ice and ice-cream for sale, announcing at the same time that someone had arrived from the mountains in the interior with a supply of this article, which was son converted into excellent cream.

Guayaquil is supplied with great quantities of excellent fruit, common to tropical regions. Pineapples are very abundant and cheap, as are oranges, bananas and plantains. Water and musk melons are also cheap and plenty. The beef and mutton, as in most other hot climates, is indifferent, and the beef appears even worse than it otherwise would do, in consequence of the slovenly manner of cutting it up. They do not dress it as in other countries, but tear and cut the flesh from off the bone of the animal in strings, and sell it by the yard or *vara*. As this is the first and only place in which I ever bought beef by the yard, I thought it worthy of notice in my narrative.

About noon, on the 31st of August, the captain of the brig *Los dos Hermanos* sent me word that he was ready for sea, and wished all his passengers to repair on board forthwith. Not having much baggage to look after, I took leave of the few friends I had in Guayaquil, and hurried on board. On our way to the brig, we passed through the market and purchased a large quantity of fruit for sea-stores. Among other things, I purchased some twenty or thirty large water-melons, which I found preferable to every kind of fruit. I never shall forget how gratefully refreshing we found them on a hot, calm morning, under a vertical sun, with the ther. at 85° above zero.

We did not leave the town until 3 o'clock in the afternoon; and, as the wind was light and variable, we drifted slowly down the river with the ebb tide, until about 10 o'clock, when it became quite dark, and we anchored for the night. Here again I was pleased with what to me was a novel occurrence. Far away to the eastward, in the interior, I saw a great light and innumerable sparks of fire, which illuminated the sky, so as to render the scene vivid and beautiful. Upon inquiry, I found it was a burning volcano, at a great distance in the interior. It appeared to be some thirty or forty miles distant, while it was, in fact, perhaps fifty leagues off.

The next morning, at daylight, September 1st, we got under way, and made a short cut to the sea, through a passage to the northward of the island of Puna. Our brig drew very little water, and we were therefore able to pass through small rivers and creeks where larger vessels dare not venture.

I soon discovered that our captain was a vain, ignorant, superstitious man, and knew nothing of navigation. He had neither chart nor quadrant on board. Fortunately for us, however, our *contramaéstre*, or boatswain, was a good seaman and an excellent pilot. He was a native of Old Spain, and although deficient in education, was a discreet, respectable man. He disciplined and managed the crew, and left little or nothing for the captain to do, but eat, drink, smoke, and sleep. The man was only an apology for a captain, and was in the habit of following the land along shore on his voyages between Guayaquil and Panama; whereby, in lieu of making a straight course, he prolonged his passage to double the number of days necessary. I had with me a quadrant and many charts of the western coast, from Guayaquil to Panama, on a large scale, and politely pointed out to him the true and straight course. I say politely, for I have ever found, that with the ignorant and superstitious of all nations, the greatest possible caution and delicacy must be observed when advising them, otherwise their self-love and jealousy take fire, and they become your enemies.

This vulgar captain at first inclined to adhere to his own opinion,—said he had navigated this part of the coast for many years, and always with success, and was afraid of sudden changes. His countrymen, the two passengers, however, fell in with me and persuaded him to follow my advice, and endeavour to shorten the distance of the passage. The two passengers alluded to were merchants, or shop-keepers, who visited Panama occasionally to purchase and sell goods, and on their way up and down, used to touch at a small place called Monte Christi, to trade, and to this place we were now bound on our way to Panama.

There were five passengers,—making, with officers and crew, a total of fifteen souls on board the *Dos Hermanos*— all of whom lived on deck, night and day, except the two Guayaquil traders and myself. The *contramaéstre* had the entire management of the vessel, and appeared to be always on the watch, both by night and day. The sailors were not divided into watches, as is the custom on board of vessels of other nations, but all slept in the long-boat on deck, on a dry ox hide, with another spread over them. Whenever it was necessary to make or take in sail, they were all called; and when the work was done all lay down to sleep again. They appeared to work with alacrity, and were always ready to obey the boatswain without grumbling. We had been out but a few days before we encountered much hot, rainy weather. At these times our situation, in the little hole of a cabin, was deplorable. When it rained violently, a large tarpaulin was spread over the companion-way to keep the cabin dry.— On such occasions, particularly in the night, the captain and the deck passengers would crawl in for shelter, and I was often obliged to leave my berth, and struggle through the crowd to get a little air at the door to prevent suffocation.

We were provided with only two meals a day; the first, called breakfast, about 11 o'clock in the forenoon, was taken always on deck. This meal was either a *fricassee* or *puchero*, with bread and a little common, low Catalonia wine. The other meal we generally had at four or five o'clock in the afternoon, and it was composed of about the same in quality, served up in one large dish placed in the centre of the quarterdeck. Our polite captain always helped himself first, and then advised everybody to do the like. The food of the sailors on the main-deck consisted of plantain and *charque* or dried beef. Thus situated, we passed some days, creeping along at a slow pace, and making but little progress on our course, with variable winds, and very hot, calm weather.

On Sunday morning, September 5th, at daylight in the morning, we ran into the little bay of Monte Christi, and came to anchor very near the shore, in three fathoms of water.

This is a clean little bay, with a fine sand beach, and a few small houses, called *ranchos* and shops, at the landing. The town of Monte Christi is located three or four miles inland from the port, in an easterly direction. This lonely little harbour lies in lat. 1° 1' S., long. 80° 32' W. of London. It was quite destitute of shipping, there being no vessel there except our little brig. We procured horses from the *rancheros* at the landing, and soon galloped over a pleasant road, to the town. It being Sunday morning, the whole town, or as the French say, "*tout le monde*," were decked out in their holiday dresses. Our captain and the two Guayaquil traders had planned a great deal of business for the day, and were very impatient to attend mass, that they might proceed to its execution afterwards. Accordingly, we left our horses at a poor little *posada*, and then hurried to the church. I went with them near the door, and after having excused myself for leaving them, took a stroll about the town. Everybody appeared to be on the move towards the church, arrayed in gaudy dresses, of bright red and yellow colours. These simple people seemed as fond of displaying their gay attire as children decked out in their holiday suits.

After a little survey of the town, I entered a house for some water, when the following dialogue occurred between the master of the house and myself. After presenting me with a chair and giving me a welcome reception, he said, "I suppose you landed this morning from the brigantine, on your way to Panama?"

"Yes, I did so," I replied.

"The captain and the passengers have all gone to mass, how is it that you did not go also—are you not a Christian?"

I answered I was, but having a very imperfect knowledge of the Spanish language, I preferred walking about the town. I then took the same liberty with him, and inquired why he did not go. He replied that he attended early mass, and was always very attentive to his religious duties. He then questioned me on the religious faith and belief of my countrymen in England. I told him I was not from that country, but from North America. He then called me an *Anglo-Americano*, and seemed to have a confused idea that we were the descendants of the English. and lived in a distant region of which very little was known, and inquired whether our belief and faith was the same as that of the English; that he had always been told that the English were all heretics and unbelievers. I told him that the religion of the two countries was about the same, that neither of them were heretics or unbelievers. He expressed great surprise, and then asked me if we believed in *"el Padre et Hijo y el Espiritu Santo."*

On my answering him in the affirmative, he appeared still more astonished, and said, then he had always been greatly deceived, that he had from his childhood been told by the priests and friars that the English were all infidels, and did not believe in the Trinity, nor yet in the "Holy Mother of God, the pure and holy Virgin Mary." I then told him there was certainly a great difference between the belief of his countrymen and mine, on the subject of worship due to the Virgin Mary, and holy reverence to a great many saints, but that the greater part of the churches, both in England and North America, professed to believe in the Trinity. He appeared very well satisfied with my explanation,— and said he had no doubt we had been misrepresented and slandered; and that he would inquire further into the subject from the first intelligent Englishman he should meet.

While I am on this subject, I will relate an anecdote that occurred one evening at the lodgings of Captain O'Sullivan, while I was at Guayaquil. Among other questions, the mistress of the house, a middle-aged, good looking lady, asked me whether there were any Jews in my country. I told her there were many. She then asked me what they looked like, and whether they had tails. I was for a moment surprised, and thought she was jesting, and hardly knew how to answer,—when she observed, that she had always been told that Jews were strange-looking creatures, and had long tails like cows hanging down behind them. She said she came to Guayaquil about two years before, from a village in the interior of Colombia, and that from her infancy she had been always told by the priests, that Jews had tails, and were odious, frightful-looking creatures. I was astonished at her simple ignorance, for she was not one of the lower order, but a woman of polite manners, and spoke the Spanish language with ease and grace.

I have related these two incidents from a thousand other similar ones, that have come under my observation while travelling about South America, not with a view of exposing the ignorance of these honest, simple-hearted people, as objects of ridicule, but to hold up to the world the wickedness of these vile priests and friars, who delude and darken the minds of unfortunate beings, who are the subjects of their cunning priest-craft. In the United States we abhor the military despot who enslaves and chains the body; but is not the man who darkens and enslaves the mind, ten times more guilty than the military despot? I can overlook with some degree of patience a great many faults and superstitious prejudices in the uneducated and ignorant, but have very little patience or charity for these vile leaders of the blind, who know better than to prey upon the ignorance and credulity of their fellow-men, either in matters of church or state. The wicked policy of keeping mankind in ignorance, in order to profit by their want of knowledge, cannot but excite the indignation of him who loves his fellow-man.

Monte Christi is situated on an undulating surface, moderately high, with one considerable church located on rising ground, in the centre of the town, which probably contains about 1500 inhabitants. The houses are generally one story high, and are built of sun-dried brick; some, however, are two stories, and have tile roofs.

The weather here is so hot that the inhabitants keep within doors during the middle of the day. In the evening it becomes cool and pleasant. This town and its vicinity, like most other places near the equator, are subject to periodical wet and dry seasons. During the heavy rains, many of the people remove to the hills, taking their cattle and other domestic animals along with them; and at the commencement of the dry season, return to their former habitations. I understood that the dry seasons last from December to April, and the wet during the rest of the year.

My stay here was so short that I could collect little reliable information on the subject of the general state of this country. I found the people generally a mixed breed of Spaniard, Indian, and *Mulatto*.

Our captain and the two Guayaquil traders, after mass on the day of our arrival here, arranged their commercial affairs with the principal shop-keepers of the town, and when we had partaken of a tolerable dinner at the little *posada*, we all mounted our horses about 4 o'clock in the afternoon, and returned again to the port. Here we landed several bags of cocoa, and a quantity of boxes of merchandise; and took on board some dry hides, and eight or ten bags of dollars; and after renewing our sea-stores of plantain and livestock, got under way just before dark, and steered out of the bay on our course for Panama.

I learned from the two Guayaquil traders, that they were in the habit of leaving goods with the shop-keepers at Monte Christi, to dispose of for their account, and always stopped on their way up and down from Panama to Guayaquil, to receive the amount of what they had sold, either in money or in the produce of the country. I was surprised at the amount of the cargo and money transported in this trifling little craft. I think one of these gentlemen told me there was about $30,000 on board of our little brig, besides other valuable articles, which we were now taking to Panama, with which to pay debts and purchase merchandise for Guayaquil and the western coast of Colombia. I am thus minute on the subject of this small trading vessel, to show that although a craft of this description would not be considered capable or safe to make a sea voyage along the coast of the States, here the mild winds and smooth seas do not endanger almost any kind of vessel that will float, whilst trading along the coast between Guayaquil and Panama.

During the night there was a pleasant little breeze from off the land, and the next day, we had light and variable winds, with fine weather. At noon, I amused myself, while sailing along shore, by taking a meridian observation; and it so happened that the sun at noon was vertical, or directly over head, and I could therefore sweep his image with the quadrant all round the horizon, and fully realize that we were on the equator, and consequently in no latitude. Our longitude at this time was about 80° 00' W. from London.

We continued to have light and variable winds, with occasional showers, for several days after crossing the equator. The weather during the daytime was generally very warm, and we had little or nothing to screen us from the rays of the sun, in this small and very uncomfortable vessel. Our captain, as I have before said, was an ignorant, ill-bred man, and took no pains to secure the comfort or convenience of his passengers; —these evils rendered the time extremely tedious. We had, however, got about three degrees to the northward of the line, and were now making a pretty straight course for Panama. By the persuasion of the passengers and myself, our captain consented to steer boldly on our course to the northward, and not to follow the land along the whole length of Chuco bay, as he was inclined to do. He had neither chart nor quadrant on board,—and upon reflection, I was not surprised that he should not venture far out of sight of *terra firma*. The *contramaéstre* was a good seaman and an excellent fellow; and frankly acknowledged that he knew nothing of navigation, though he was well acquainted with the land, and could navigate up and down the coast almost by instinct. As we increased our latitude to the northward, the winds gradually freshened, and we got on without any material accident.

On the morning of the 16th of Sept., 1822, we made Point St. Francisco Solano, and the land to the eastward of the entrance of the bay of Panama. Point St. Francisco Solano is a prominent headland, and lies in lat. 6° 49' N., long. 77° 47' W. We steered up to the northward, keeping in sight of the land on the eastern side of the bay, and found the coast clear and easy to navigate. During the night the wind was light. The next day, Sept. 17th, we made several islands lying in this beautiful bay,—and as the weather was fine and the sea smooth, it was very pleasant sailing among the islands. We steered to the northward, and now had land on both sides of the bay. On passing the islands, we saw several men in boats employed in catching pearl oysters. The shells, I believe, are here not of much value, though considerable quantities are occasionally shipped from Panama to England.

The next day, September 18th, we came to anchor off the town of Panama; and in a few minutes after went on shore, and forever bade *adieu* to our captain and the brig *Los Dos Hermanos*.

I was, of course, delighted to get on shore at Panama; but I was not a little disappointed to find the city so badly supplied with hotels. Although there were two or three tolerable cafés, where one could get something to eat and drink, still, I believe, there was not a good hotel in the place. I was told that the best way of living there, was to hire a room or two, and then get a black woman to cook. I accordingly hired a few rooms for myself and my two young friends, and engaged a black woman to dress our food and keep the rooms in order. In this way we got along tolerably well, and without any great expense.

To my satisfaction, I met here Captain John Brown, of the schooner *Freemason,* of Baltimore. This schooner was lying at Chagrés, and Captain Brown expected to sail for the Havana in about a fortnight. I engaged a passage with him for myself and the two young gentlemen who came with me from Guayaquil.

The *Freemason* was the only American vessel lying at Chagrés; and we deemed ourselves fortunate in meeting with so good an opportunity to return to the United States, by way of the Havana.

Captain Brown soon introduced me to his consignee, J. B. Ferand, Esq., the American consul at this place. I found Mr. Ferand to be a polite, obliging, gentlemanly man, and he was to me always a kind friend.

As it was quite healthy at Panama, and very sickly at Chagrés, I concluded to remain in the former city until the *Freemason* was ready for sea; and not having any business to do, I had sufficient leisure to walk about the town and its vicinity, and view the Key of the Isthmus, as Panama is sometimes called.

The city of Panama lies at the head of a fine broad bay, of the same name, sprinkled with islands sheltering the harbour, and beautifying the surrounding scenery. It lies in lat. 8° 59' N., and long. 79° 22' W.; and like most other towns built by the Spaniards, is strongly walled and tolerably well fortified. It belongs to the republic of Colombia, and contains about ten or twelve thousand inhabitants. The streets are generally regular— and many of the houses are commodious and well built. Some of the public buildings are large and substantial, particularly the cathedral and several convents, and also the college. The college of the Jesuits, however, is now but a ruin. The environs of the town are pleasant, and the grounds in the neighbourhood tolerably well cultivated. It was once a great place for trade, but had, during the last twenty or thirty years, gradually declined in its commerce. There was however, some little trade still carried on; and should a canal or a railroad be constructed across the isthmus, Panama will revive again. The natural position of the city is excellent,—and it will, in my opinion, at some future day, become a place of considerable importance.

The tide rises here to a great height—(I do not recollect precisely how many feet)—at the full and change of the moon, but as near as I can remember, some eighteen or twenty feet. Large vessels anchor at a considerable distance from the town, and lie afloat at low water; the small coasting vessels anchor close in near the walls of the city, and consequently lie on the mud at low water. The inner harbour is quite dry; the sand and mud flats extend off to a great distance, which at low tide give to the harbour an unpleasant aspect; but at the flood, the tide rises rapidly; the mud and sand banks are soon covered, and the whole scene agreeably changed from dreary banks to a living sheet of healthful salt-water.

It often struck me while strolling about this town, how admirably it was situated for a great commercial city; with a wide and extensive coast,—one may even say, from Cape Horn to Behring's Straits—with innumerable islands in the vast Pacific Ocean—with an open and easy navigation to China, over a sea so mild and gentle, that it might almost be traversed in an open boat. All these facilities are open to this town on the Pacific; and when we add to these its capacities of a general commerce on the Atlantic Ocean to Europe, the United States, and the West Indies, its location surpasses every other on the face of the globe. And now, what is necessary to bring about this great result? I answer—a just and good government, with a few enterprising capitalists, and five hundred young men from New England to give the impetus. Whaling ships—merchant ships trading to China—coasting brigs, schooners, sloops, and steamboats, would spring up like mushrooms; and in a few years this place would become one of the greatest commercial emporiums in the world.

A practical intelligent merchant, acquainted with the commerce of the world, will see by a glance at the map, that I have stated nothing respecting it either unreal or extravagant.

A few days before we left Panama, Captain Brown made an arrangement with the municipal government of this place, or perhaps with an agent of the republic of Colombia, to take as passengers about eighty Spanish prisoners and their colonel, from Chagrés to the Havana, and also a Colombian officer, by the name of Barientes (I think he was a major), to take charge of the businesses commissioner.

These Spanish prisoners, I understood, capitulated at Quito, on the conditions that they should leave the country and be sent to the Havana in a neutral vessel, at the expense of the Spanish government. The Colombian government agreed to furnish them with provisions, and pay Captain Brown a certain sum to land them at the Havana; I think it was about $1800 or $2000. This money was paid in advance at Chagrés.

Captain Brown had now so far accomplished his business, that I began to make my arrangements to leave Panama; and for that purpose, hired a guide and five mules to transport Messrs. B. C. and A. D., my two young American friends, myself and our baggage to Cruces. For the guide and the five mules, I paid forty-two dollars;—and thus, after remaining at Panama fourteen days, on the 2nd of October, at 4 o'clock in the afternoon, we left the city for Cruces. We travelled slowly along— myself and the two young men mounted on the riding mules (the other two were loaded with our baggage), the guide generally walking, in order to pick the best of the road and take care of the mules. He, however, rode occasionally on one of the baggage mules. The road for three or four miles after leaving the city was tolerably good, or rather the different footpaths, for I saw nothing like a road on the whole route from Panama to Cruces. From Panama to the foot of the hills—a distance of about five or six miles—there is a gradual elevation, and nothing to prevent making a good road at a small expense.

We passed over this part of the way rather pleasantly, and just before dark took up our abode for the night in a miserable *posada*, where neither a bed nor anything eatable could be obtained. I got liberty to spread my mattress on the floor,—my young friends had each a blanket with them, and we all lay down in the same room; and though thus badly accommodated, were glad to get shelter for the night.

At daylight, our guide called us to mount the mules and make the best of our way. Our bedding was soon rolled up and packed on one of the animals; and we resumed our journey over one of the worst roads I ever travelled—up and down hill, through mud-holes, and over stony ground. Sometimes we met with large stones lying in the mud and sand, that had been washed out of the earth and not removed. Over these stones, many of which were the size of a barrel, we were obliged to pass. At other times the mules would mire above their knees, in passing through a deep slough. After getting through a low spot of mud and water, the next turn would bring us to a cut in the rocks, just wide enough for a loaded mule to pass. These passes are frequently made through the solid rocks; and as they have probably been used a century and a half, the mules' feet have worn large holes, and these are generally filled with water, so that the poor animals, whether going through the mud, slough, or rocky pass, have a difficult task to perform.

On the way, we frequently met with men carrying valuable goods on their backs, to and from Panama to Cruces. Almost all fragile and valuable goods are conveyed across the Isthmus by porters on their backs: such as China and glassware, clocks, and other merchandise. Coarser and heavier goods are transported by mules. During the day, we occasionally saw huts and small *ranchos* along the roadside, mostly inhabited by a miserable, sickly-looking set of creatures, a mixed breed of the Spaniard, Indian, and Negro.

There is very little cultivation of the soil. The hills and valleys are generally well wooded and watered, but in a wild, savage state; and the people that vegetate here, live by raising cattle, pigs and poultry, and are extremely filthy and ignorant. The porters that convey goods on their backs from Cruces to Panama, are paid, I was told, from five to six dollars each way. The labour, however, is extremely severe, and none but the most hardy can long endure the fatigue.

We could scarcely get anything to eat on the road, and did not arrive at Cruces until late in the afternoon, and then very much worn down with fatigue. Although the distance from Panama to Cruces is only twenty-one miles, the journey is tedious from the badness of the roads.

Cruces is a small town,—consisting of some eighty or a hundred little houses, lying on the west bank of the river Chagrés, about fifty miles above its mouth, at the head of navigation. The houses are one story high, and generally built of wood with thatched roofs. The ground on which the town is situated is pretty level, and about twenty feet above the river. We found here comfortable accommodations, and had a good night's rest, after the fatigue of a long day's ride.

The next morning, the weather being fine, I walked about the town. The inhabitants are generally shopkeepers and boatmen, with a small proportion of mechanics. As Captain Brown was still in Panama, I was in no hurry to push on, being told that this place was more healthy and pleasant than Chagrés. His clerk, a young Spanish gentlemen, whose name was Francisco, joined us here, and was a friendly, polite young man, and very companionable. During the day I hired a boat, or rather a large canoe, and four men to take us down to Chagrés;—we were to furnish our own stores. The canoes on this river are very large and long. They are made by hollowing out a solid tree of Spanish cedar. Some of them carry over one hundred half barrels of flour. Whole barrels of flour are rarely brought to Chagrés, owing to the difficulty of transporting them from Cruces to Panama. The canoe I hired for myself, and the three other passengers was of middle size, and the price agreed upon to take us down was thirteen dollars. After having purchased stores for the passage, we got a good dinner and remained at Cruces until near sunset, when we embarked.

The canoes have hoops of bamboo bent over the after part of the craft, which is covered with a water-tight awning, so that the passengers are sheltered from the sun by day, and the dews and rain by night. With our mattresses and blankets spread in the stern sheets, we managed to sleep pretty well during the night. The river is not very wide, but generally deep and extremely crooked, and runs down very rapidly. I should think it from a quarter to half a mile wide. Its banks are generally abrupt, and from thirty to fifty feet high. Near the river, the wood is frequently cleared off, with now and then a little village, or a few small plantations; but receding a mile or two from the river, it appears like a vast wild forest, and a suitable habitation for wild beasts. In these jungles one would imagine they could remain undisturbed by the slothful race of men who inhabit the isthmus. The trees here grow to an enormous size, and vegetation is rank and green all the year round.

Our lazy boatmen knew that we were not in a hurry, and therefore let the canoe drift down the stream pretty much all night, without rowing. Early in the morning we stopped at a small village, and bought some eggs and milk for breakfast; after remaining here about an hour, we pulled slowly down with the current. Soon after midday we brought up again at a small landing place, purchased a few trifling articles, and took our dinner under the shade of a fine large old tree on the bank of the river. This was on the 5th of October, and at 2 o'clock in the afternoon we re-embarked and pulled down for our port of destination. At nightfall it became dark and foggy, and we did not reach Chagrés until 9 o'clock in the evening. As there was no hotel on shore, we went directly to the vessel, and had scarcely got on board and taken out our baggage, before it commenced raining, and continued to pour in torrents during the whole night. From 10 o'clock till midnight we had loud peals of thunder, and vivid lightning.

At daylight it ceased raining, but there was a dense vapour like fog until about nine o'clock in the morning, when the sun shone out, and as there was not a breath of wind, it was extremely hot and uncomfortable, and the exhalations were so dense and bad that we found it difficult to breathe the foul atmosphere. This was on the 6th of October. Chagrés is a small insignificant village, lying on low wet ground, along the eastern bank of the river's mouth, in lat. 9°. 21' N., long. 80° 4' W., of London. To the windward, or eastern entrance of the river, there is a point of land of moderate height, projecting somewhat into the sea, and forming a shelter for vessels lying at anchor in the mouth of the river, which here widens so as to form a sort of harbour; this, together with the bar at the entrance, renders it a safe port from all gales of wind. To the leeward, and along the western bank of the river, the land is low, and overgrown with rank grass, and high mangrove bushes.

At 10 o'clock, notwithstanding the sun was shining with intense heat, I went on shore to take a look at the village, or town. We soon brought up in a *pulperia* or grog-shop, which appeared to be the only resort for strangers, there being no hotel or tavern in this miserable place.

On the eastern point before mentioned, there is a small fort, at which, and about the town, there is a military garrison of perhaps thirty or forty sickly-looking soldiers. They are mostly *mulatto*es and negroes, badly clothed, and worse fed. The commanding officer of this little garrison, and the great man of the place, was a middle-sized *mulatto*, about thirty or thirty-five years old. Captain Brown's clerk, Mr. Francisco, told me we had better call on the commandant or captain of the garrison; that he no doubt expected all strangers to pay their respects to him on their arrival. This I was quite willing to do, and by all means to treat the public authorities with all proper respect and attention. We therefore forthwith repaired to the house of the commandant; we found him comfortably lodged in good quarters, and we were received with much ceremony. The commandant was dressed in full uniform, with two immense *epaulettes*, and assumed an air of consequential dignity; he offered us wine, and made a great flourish of male and female attendants. This visit of ceremony lasted about half an hour, when we took leave, the commandant politely bowing us out of his premises.

The schooner *Freemason* was the only American vessel lying in port; there were two or three others, and these small coasting vessels which are employed trading up and down the coast.

Both of the mates and two of the seamen of our vessel were ill with the yellow fever, and hardly able to keep the deck; and here we were to remain for several days, to wait for our passengers and their stores, which were to be furnished by the Colombian government, and also to be brought from Panama. The stores for the eighty Spanish prisoners consisted of *charque*, plantain, and a small portion of hard biscuit. The colonel and commissioner were better provided, and were to mess with Captain Brown and myself in the cabin. Captain Brown had agreed to furnish water, and the poor sick mates, who were hardly able to crawl about the deck, were endeavouring, with a few sailors, to get all the water casks filled up from the river before the captain should arrive.

Previous to leaving Guayaquil, I became acquainted with an elderly intelligent Spaniard, who had been for many years at Porto Bello and Chagrés; he told me by all means to wear woollen stockings or socks during the time I remained at Chagrés, and to bathe my feet two or three times a day with brandy or some other kind of alcohol, and by no means expose myself to the night air or noonday sun. I strictly followed the old man's advice while I remained here, and have to thank him, with God's blessing, that I escaped taking the fever. I enjoyed excellent health during my stay at Chagrés, which is, perhaps, the most sickly place on the face of the globe.

During the day, I observed the clouds were driven by the N.E. trade-winds, and were collecting and hanging above and about the hills and mountains in the neighbourhood, and I may also add all along the northern coast of the isthmus; towards night they lay in immense masses, and appeared, as it were, to rest on the tops of the lofty forest trees, which crown these high hills and mountains. Soon after sunset we began to see the lightning, and hear the thunder above the mountains, and it was kept up with increasing fury until about 9 or 10 o'clock in the evening, when the rains began to fall in perfect sheets of water.

I have witnessed copious showers in other countries, but nothing to compare with the torrents that fell here during the night; I have also seen it lighten and heard it thunder in other parts of the world, but never saw or heard anything to equal what I nightly witnessed in this place. Peal after peal rends the air, and, to a stranger, throws an appalling gloom over this doomed portion of the earth. In the morning about ten o'clock the sun broke out as on the previous day, and I found it difficult and dangerous to go on shore without an umbrella to protect me from the rays of the burning sun.

As the history of one day is exactly that of another, I deem it unnecessary to say much more on the monotonous life I led. With respect to the weather, it continued about the same during my stay, a bright burning sun during the day, with torrents of rain during the night, accompanied with vivid lightning and thunder.

Although it is very easy to descend the river Chagrés in a large canoe, well protected from the sun by day, and the dews and rain by night, it is not so easy to ascend it against a very rapid current running from three to six miles an hour, according to the high or low stage of the water. Loaded canoes are often a week getting from Chagrés to Cruces: the men are obliged to track up the stream, and with boat-hooks haul up along shore by the trees and bushes.

To convey passengers, the light canoes are taken, and they generally make the passage in two days. If asked whether there is sufficient water in the river for a steamboat, I would answer that I believe there is, and no obstruction but want of sufficient employment to support the expense of a boat. At this time there were very few passengers crossing the isthmus, and too little trade to give any encouragement to establishing a steamboat on the river.

On the 8th of October Captain Brown arrived, with the Spanish colonel and the commissioner, Major Barientes, with all the sea-stores, both for the Spanish soldiers and the officers, and now all was hurry and bustle getting ready for sea. The next day, Oct. 9th, I called with Captain Brown to pay our respects to the *mulatto* commandant, and to take a memorandum of this man in authority to purchase whatever he should please to order from Baltimore. Captain Brown had already made two or three voyages from Baltimore to this place; and as he expected to return there again in a few months, he of course had a great many little commissions to execute for the elite of Panama and Chagrés. On our arrival at the quarters of the commandant, we found him decked off in a new suit of gaudy uniform,—and here I witnessed a ludicrous farce between Captain Brown and the *mulatto* major. The latter was a vain and conceited coxcomb, evidently bent on showing off and playing the great man. Captain Brown was a plain, blunt Scotchman, and understood not a word of Spanish, but was endowed with a good understanding, and was by nature kind and benevolent. Independent of these qualities, it was his interest to keep smooth weather, and be upon good terms with the major;—he therefore waited with patience to receive the orders of the gallant commandant. I lament that I possess not the graphic powers of Dr. Smollett to describe the ludicrous.

Captain Brown's secretary, Mr. F., was seated at a table with pen, ink and paper, to note down the orders of the *mulatto* gentleman, who, to show his learning, endeavoured to give his directions in phrases of bad French, interlarded with a few words of English. He would now and then walk about the room for a few moments, and admire himself, from head to foot, in a large mirror suspended at the head of the room. Mr. F. modestly requested him to give his orders in the Castilian language; but this plain dealing did not suit the taste of the major, who reproved him for his presumption, and then would reverse the order and direct him to commence anew, and strictly follow the orders given in his own way. The animated gesticulations and pomposity of the yellow major, and the unmoved indifference of the captain, formed so striking a contrast, that it was with the greatest difficulty I could command my risible faculties. This farce lasted about an hour, when we took our leave of "*señor commandant*," and left him to admire himself without interruption.

I can only imagine one reason why the Colombian Government should place such a vain fool in the command of so important a post, and that is, that the place is so unhealthy that no white man could live there.

Oct. 11th.—At 9 o'clock in the morning we weighed anchor, and with the boat ahead to tow, and a light air off the land, sailed out of the harbour bound to the Havana. After getting a mile or two from the river's mouth, it became quite calm. There we lay exposed to the hot sun for two hours, waiting for the sea breeze, to beat up to windward far enough to stand to the northward, and thus clear the land to the westward, and make good our course out of the bay.

The schooner *Freemason* was a good vessel, of about 100 tons burthen, and a pretty fair sailer. In the cabin were the captain, the Spanish colonel, Major Barientes; and myself. In the steerage were the two sick mates, and the two young men that came with me from Guayaquil. The main-hold was left for the Spanish soldiers. Two of the crew in the forecastle were ill with the yellow fever, and the mates unfit for duty, and, notwithstanding all these evils, we were delighted to leave Chagrés for the broad ocean, and once more to breath the pure sea air, and thus fly from pestilence and death.

At 11 o'clock, after lying becalmed two hours, a breeze sprung up from the E. N. E., when we commenced beating up to windward; and just at sunset, after having made fifteen or twenty miles up along shore, we steered to the N. N. E. all night with a stiff trade-wind from the east, and the next day, Oct. 11th, at 4 p. m., made the island of St Andrew. This island lies off the Mosquito shore, in lat. 12° 30' N., long. 81° W.. After passing this island we kept the trade-wind, and as it was light, we made but little progress during the night. At 6 a. m., soon after daylight, we made the island of Providence. This island is of a moderate height, and lies in lat. 13° 27' N., long. 80° 39'

W. of London; distant about sixty miles to the northward of St. Andrew. We ran within a mile or two of Providence, namely, to the westward, or in seamen's phrase, under the lee of the island. Thus we continued on our course to the northward, and passed to the windward of the numerous small islands, reefs, and shoals, lying off the coast of the Mosquito shore.

Just at night on this day, Oct. 13th (sea account), Captain Brown was taken very ill, and unable to come on deck; the second mate sick below, and the chief mate, poor fellow, so reduced from the effect of the fever contracted in Chagrés that he was with difficulty able to keep the deck during the day. We were now in a dangerous and very difficult situation, surrounded with reefs and shoals, and no one to take the command of the vessel. The old Spanish colonel and Major Barientes saw our situation, and begged me for God's sake to take the command of the schooner. I was placed in a very delicate position; but under all the circumstances of the case, consented to do so. I mustered all the men in the forecastle, well enough to keep watch, and they numbered two. With these, and my two New York friends, and the cook, I took command of the schooner; and as the weather was dark and squally, I kept the deck all night, beating about in the passage until daylight, when we again got a strong trade-wind from E. N. E., and fine, clear, pleasant weather. We were now clear of all the reefs and shoals, and made a fair wind for Cape Antonio, on the west end of Cuba. At 10 o'clock in the morning, Captain Brown was better, and able to come on deck and resume the command of the schooner.

The Spanish colonel was a gentlemanly man of about sixty. He had been in the armies in South America seven or eight years, and in many severe engagements, and always fought with honour to himself and to his country; but was beaten at last at the battle of Quito, where he and many of his countrymen laid down their arms and capitulated to be sent out of the country. He was indeed a war-worn soldier, and I fear had been poorly remunerated for his hard and severe sufferings. He was a kind, amiable man, with very modest and unassuming manners, and won the respect and esteem of all those about him.

Major Barientes, the commissioner, was a fine, healthy looking young man, about thirty or thirty-five years of age; he had been several years in the Colombian service, and I have no doubt was a gallant fellow, and was now on his way to a colony of Spain, to deliver the colonel and the Spanish soldiers up to the government of Cuba, and claim from it the money and the fulfilment of the capitulation made at the battle of Quito.

I was often amused with the conversation of these two gentlemen on the subject of the different battles fought in South America between their respective countrymen, each, of course, endeavouring to make his own countrymen superior and victorious. Generally their conversations and recitals were carried on in a good spirit; sometimes, however, they would wax a little warm in these little disputes. I good-naturedly reminded them that here we were all friends together, and had no fighting to do; this always brought them to a just sense of their relative situations, when their arguments would take a gentle tone, and end in mutual good wishes that the war between Spain and her colonies might soon terminate. I found them both well-bred and agreeable fellow-passengers.

The mates and seamen were now convalescent, and everything went on smoothly, and in a few days we made Cape St. Antonio, and proceeded on our course without any incident worth remarking, until off Mariel, the day before we arrived at Havana. Here we fell in with a Spanish sloop of war, ship-rigged, and mounting eighteen guns. She ranged up near us, and seeing so many men on our decks, either took us for a privateer or a pirate. Her guns were pointed, and everything ready to give us a broadside, although so near that she could, no doubt, see we had no guns. Our captain expected every moment to receive her fire. We were lying to when she hailed and ordered us to send our boat on board instantly, or she would sink us. We had but one boat, and it was dried up with the sun, so that the moment it touched the water it leaked like a sieve. Still the order was imperative and must be obeyed. Captain Brown requested the colonel and myself to go on board, and show him the schooner's papers. We got into the boat, and, with constant bailing, made out to get on board of the ship, though not in a very good condition, being wet up to our knees. We showed our papers to the captain, who was a very young man, and, after a little delay, we were requested to take seats on the quarter-deck.

The colonel explained the substance of the capitulation, his misfortunes, &c. &c. The captain appeared rather to upbraid than sympathize with the good colonel, who was old enough to be his father. I felt, vexed with the upstart. Our visit was of short duration. The captain of the ship neither invited the veteran to take a glass of wine, nor any other refreshment, nor was he at all polite. I sincerely regret I do not recollect the name of this worthy old warrior, who bore such treatment with so much patience.

While in the boat, I observed to the colonel that his countryman, the captain of the ship, did not treat him with the consideration and courtesy due to his rank and misfortunes. He mildly replied that he was a very young man, and was probably promoted by family interest, and had little sympathy for the unfortunate.

The ship soon made sail, and we steered on our course, and the next day, October 28th, came to anchor at Havana, eighteen days from Chagrés. The health-boat soon came alongside, and we were allowed to go on shore.

Major Barientes went on shore in full Colombian uniform, and, I was told, was well received by the governor, but whether he ever recovered the money due to his government, I have never been able to learn. I took a kind farewell of these two worthy gentlemen, and we never again met.

I was very anxious to get home, and as there was no vessel to sail soon for New York, engaged a passage to Philadelphia, on board the hermaphrodite brig *James Coulter*, to sail the next day. I advanced a small sum of money to my young protégés, taking their orders on their friends in New York for the money I had already paid for their passages and other expenses, and left them under the protection of the American Consul at this place.

The next day we got under way, and sailed out of the harbour, bound for Philadelphia. I regret I do not recollect the name of the young man who commanded the *James Coulter*, he was an active, capable ship-master, and a worthy man. I had the good fortune to meet on board the *James Coulter*, an old friend, Captain Frazer, of Baltimore, and as we were the only passengers on board, we were very happy to meet each other, and renew our former acquaintance. We had formerly met in Europe, and now, after many years separation, it was delightful to make a passage together. I do not recollect anything remarkable during our passage home. Everything went on in perfect good order, and we had a very pleasant passage of only fifteen days to the city of Philadelphia.

I think I paid $50 for my passage, and was well satisfied with both the vessel and the captain. We landed in the afternoon of the 14th of November, 1822, and the next day I took the steamboat for New York, and arrived in that city at noon, the next day following, after an absence of just twelve months.

I had not received a syllable from home during my long and tedious absence, and was extremely anxious to hear from my family and friends, and therefore with precipitation I hurried to the counting-office of my friend. I met my friend B., and not a word was spoken, but I saw in his face that I was doomed to be a miserable man, and that I was bereft of the dearest object for me that earth contained. I conjured him to speak out and let me know the worst. I told him I was a man, and could bear grief. He then told me that my wife died in Brooklyn, on the 3rd of October, and was interred on the 5th, and that she had left me a fine little daughter, about seven months old.

I forthwith proceeded to my melancholy abode, and although I was stricken and cut to the soul, and bereft of her my soul held the dearest of earth's treasures, still, what could I say, but repeat the words of a man more afflicted than myself, *The Lord gave, and the Lord hath taken away, and forever blessed be his holy name.*

A few weeks after my return home, my worthy friend Richard M. Lawrence, Esq., who at this period was President of the Union Marine Insurance Company in New York, called at my house, and generously offered me a situation as inspector of ships in that company. The situation had lately been vacated, and was now offered to me with a very handsome salary. I, however, declined the kind offer of my excellent friend, with many thanks; not wishing at this time to remain long on shore.

Had my wife been spared me, I should have thankfully accepted the offer, but being bereft and disappointed in my anticipations in life, I was again cast adrift and almost alone in this world of change and disappointment.

CHAPTER 7

Voyage From New York
in the Brig *Nymph*

The *Nymph* was owned by Richard M. Lawrence, Esq., and myself, jointly, and commanded by Freegift Coggeshall, jun. We purchased this vessel in New York, on the 22nd of August, 1823, and after making some little repairs, commenced loading her on the 1st of September, with an assorted cargo of beef, pork, flour, bread, rice, and other articles of provision for Cadiz. At this period, Cadiz was besieged by a French army, commanded by the Duke of Angoulême, and blockaded by a large fleet of French men-of-war, consisting of twelve line-of-battle ships, several frigates, sloops-of-war and gun-boats, amounting, in all, to twenty sail. Most of them were generally anchored at the mouth of the harbour.

The King of Spain, Ferdinand VII., was at this time confined to Cadiz, and not allowed to leave that city; he was in fact, a state prisoner to the Cortes and to the generals commanding the armies of Spain. The principal general and commander-in-chief of the Spanish armies at this period, was Riego. Knowing that Cadiz was a strongly fortified place, I thought the town would probably hold out for several months, at least long enough to give me time to get there with a cargo of provisions before it should yield, and consequently, I predicated the success of the voyage on evading the blockade.

The *Nymph* was a good sailing brig, burthen 181 tons, or

1500 barrels. We had a. large quantity of butter and lard, and the whole invoice of the cargo amounted to $9,069. I was supercargo, having taken a young cousin of mine as captain. I also took with me Mr. Edward Brown as chief mate. Mr. Brown had been in my employ for many years as master and mate, and was fully competent to act in either capacity, being a thorough-bred seaman, and a most faithful trustworthy man. The Mr. Brown here spoken of I have frequently mentioned in my early voyages, and, in particular, on a voyage to the West Indies in the *Betsey and Polly* of New-Haven, in which vessel he was chief mate, and I was second mate. With these officers, and a crew of six men, we sailed from New York on the 10th of September, 1823. We cleared for Gibraltar, but in fact were bound for Cadiz. We had generally light and contrary winds during the greater part of the passage, and made slow progress to the eastward. Nothing remarkable occurred. Everything went on quietly, and in good order. We had an excellent crew, and good officers. The brig, it is true, leaked a little too much, and the sailors were obliged to spend a great portion of their time at the pump; still, there was no grumbling or discontent, everybody was happy and willing to do his duty cheerfully.

On the 12th of October, we made Cape St. Vincent, thirty-one days from New York. The wind was light from the southward, and the weather clear and pleasant. I hauled close in shore, and the next day made Cape St. Mary; at 11 a. m., it bore north, three or four miles distant. Lat. by obs. 36° 55' N., long. 7° 52' W. I kept close in shore during the day, and spoke several fishermen, in the hope of getting some information respecting the blockading squadron off Cadiz, but found them so stupid and ignorant, that I could obtain no reliable information. I had been several times to Cadiz, and was well acquainted with the harbour and its vicinity, and therefore resolved to rely on my own resources, and trust to good fortune and perseverance. It was blowing fresh from the westward, and by passing rapidly through the fleet, in the confusion which would be created by my sudden dash, I judged it impossible for them to fire into my vessel without doing more injury to each other than to me. On a dark night it is extremely difficult to throw shot into a small vessel, when passing rapidly through a fleet.

I cautiously approached the port, and got sight of the light-house at about one hour before midnight, and then hove to for an hour, for the moon to go down. Thus far everything appeared to favour my prospects of success. At half-past 12, midnight, it being dark and somewhat squally, I filled away and passed the light-house at 2 a. m., and soon after, let go my anchor in the inner harbour of Cadiz. Here I anxiously waited for daylight. I had seen no men-of-war at the mouth of the harbour, and began to fear that the blockade was raised, and impatiently watched the first dawn of the morning to ascertain the situation of things around me.

Morning, however, soon came, and I found myself surrounded by the French fleet; the ships-of-the-line and the frigates were at anchor off in the bay, while the sloops-of-war and gun-boats were all around us.

I was at first disappointed and vexed at my bad fortune, and observed to the captain that I feared I should never be able to profit by entering a blockaded port, as this was the second time I had been defeated in a similar attempt; the first time, in the *Sea Serpent,* we were too late entering Callao. He observed, "it was true, we have been disappointed," but, said he, "I have no doubt you will surmount every difficulty, and ultimately make a good voyage."

I thanked him for his good opinion, and observed in reply, that we should always be governed in this world by circumstances, and not repine at what had already transpired.

It soon appeared that we had arrived a little too late. We got in on the 14th of October, after a long passage of thirty-three days, and the place surrendered to the French fleet and army, about a week previous to our arrival. Ours was the second American vessel that arrived after the city fell into the hands of the French. The Baltimore pilot-boat schooner *Blucher,* arrived with a full cargo of flour, four days before us, I think two days after the blockade was raised.

We were soon visited by the health-boat, and ordered to remove up the bay to the eastward of the city, and there to perform twelve days' quarantine, although every person on board was perfectly well. To enforce the quarantine laws, a small Spanish government schooner, commanded by a lieutenant in the navy, with about thirty men, was placed in the quarantine ground to watch me, and prevent my having any communication with the shore, or any other boat or vessel, during the prescribed period of my detention.

I did not regret being placed in quarantine for a few days; on the contrary, I deemed it a privilege, under present circumstances, to delay the sale of my cargo in a glutted port. Stagnation always follows the removal of a blockade, and as extremes generally follow each other in quick succession, I knew it was my policy to wait patiently a reaction in the market.

There was a garrison of French soldiers and a large fleet to be fed, besides the inhabitants of the city, and the adjacent towns of Porto, Santa Maria, St. Lucar, and many other small towns and villages in the vicinity of the once beautiful and flourishing city of Cadiz, now broken down, spiritless, and sinking under the pressure of party dissension, priest-craft, bigotry, and foreign interference.

It is a singular fact, that in Spain, defrauding the revenue is not considered a moral wrong by a large portion of the people, and by many, rather a merit than a disgrace; they consider it as only falling in with the practice of the nation, from the king down to the petty *contrabandista*, who smuggles a pound of tobacco. This principle, sanctioned or connived at by so large a portion of the community, is, no doubt, one great cause of their degradation and approaching downfall. With the masses, the prevalent feeling is that their rulers make bad laws, and that it is a virtue to break them in every way in their power.

Among the upper classes, duplicity and intrigue are studied as a science, and though parties may disagree in other respects, they each strive in a smaller or greater degree to defraud the church and state government; still, perhaps, there is no country on earth where individual punctuality and honour are held more sacred than in Spain; this principle is carried out to an astonishing degree even among the professed *contrabandistas*.

While I was lying in this port, an American captain, from an eastern port of the United States, who was rather "green" with respect to the Spanish character, and knew not a word of the language, attempted to smuggle a considerable portion of his cargo, without the knowledge of his consignee in Cadiz. After disposing of several articles at a great profit, he grew bold, and gave his custom-house officer so small a compensation that a quarrel ensued between them; the officer, in a great rage, went on shore and informed against the captain; the custom-house search-boat came immediately off to examine the vessel, and seize all the cargo not manifested. Fortunately for the captain it was very near night, and the officers had only time to find a few trifling articles, but had made their arrangements to go off in the morning and take out all the cargo not on the manifest.

In the evening, after the custom-house boat left the vessel, the captain came on shore to the house of his consignee in a great fright, and told the whole story to Don H. I was conversing with the worthy merchant at the time, and he observed that he should be a ruined man if Mr. H. could not get him out of the scrape. Mr. H. heard the captain's story, and told him he had done very wrong to attempt smuggling on so large a scale, without any knowledge of the place or language, but directed him to keep cool and quiet, and that he would get him out of trouble—that it would necessarily cost considerable money, and he hoped it would be a good lesson for him hereafter to act more prudently.

I told the unhappy, agitated captain, to sit down and remain quiet, and leave everything in the hands of his consignee. Mr. H. rang the bell for a servant, who soon appeared, and was ordered to request Mr. ——, the head clerk of his counting-office, to come to him without delay; the order was promptly obeyed, when he sent for the chief of a gang of notorious smugglers, and told him the whole story, and observed that everything not reported on the manifest of the vessel must be taken out before daylight the next morning, and the goods all concealed in a place of perfect safety, to be forthcoming when he should require them. For a certain sum (the amount I do not now recollect) a bargain was made with this desperate man that he and his comrades should perform their part of the business in good faith. The merchant then gave the captain a note to the custom-house officer, or guard on board, to come directly to his house, and directed the captain to remain on board himself, and deliver every article of merchandise not placed on the manifest, to the smugglers.

The guard came on shore, and agreed to keep out of the way for a fair compensation, and to return on board just before daylight, and thus be ready to assist the officers of the customs to find all the contraband goods. Agreeable to promise, the smugglers took out all the goods during the night, and the next morning, when the custom-house boat went on board, they found nothing but what was regularly entered, and thus the whole affair ended without further trouble; the merchant sold the goods very well soon after, and the captain saved his vessel and cargo by this *adroit* management of his consignee.

It is absurd for a stranger or a parsimonious man to attempt smuggling in Spain. What I mean by a stranger, is a man who knows nothing of the character of the people, and attempts to cheat the officers out of their proportion of the duties. In a word, with smugglers, and even with robbers, good faith must always be observed to the letter and the spirit.

After this digression I will return to the question of right and wrong, with respect to smuggling. I have before said that it is all wrong; still, when a whole nation agrees to deceive and defraud the government, it is difficult for a stranger to stem the current. For example: I will commence with King Ferdinand VII.—The liberal party declared him to be a vile bigot and a consummate hypocrite, and that he connived with the bishops and priests to gull and rob the people; that his prime minister defrauded the nation of many millions yearly; that the high officers of state pocketed all in their power for their own private purposes; and thus this system of fraud and peculation descended down to the petty customhouse officers, who are always ready to take the smallest "gratification" in the way of fee or presents.

At this period, it was melancholy to see a whole nation divided against itself. The liberal and enlightened party leaders were obliged to fly their country. Many members of the Cortes went to Gibraltar and other places, to save their lives from the fury of the king's party. In fine, the French officers found it difficult to restrain the parties from destroying each other. Many of the best and most enlightened patriots of the country were cut off by treachery and violence; and the general cry of the ignorant, bigoted classes, by night and day, was "*Viva el Rey Fernando septimo, viva la religion catolica, viva la inquisicion, abajo hos infieles liberalis.*"

The government of France, under Louis XVIII., at this time sent a powerful army into Spain, under the command of the Duke of Angoulême, to liberate and assist Ferdinand VII. and his party of priests and bigots, and to disperse and chase away from Spain the enlightened, patriotic band, who were endeavouring to regenerate their unhappy country. Thus the little light that began to beam on this unfortunate nation was soon extinguished by the priests and ignorant classes, in combination with the old Bourbon party in France, with Louis XVIII. at its head.

At the expiration of twelve days, I got *pratique*, and was allowed to discharge my cargo. By a regulation between the French and Spanish governments, flour and provisions for the French army and navy were admitted duty free. I accordingly sold my cargo to the French commissary, and by this arrangement made a freight on the whole.

In about twenty-five days after my arrival, I had sold nearly all my cargo, and soon engaged a freight for Alvarado.—During our stay here, we had much bad weather, which is generally the case at this season of the year. Cadiz is very subject, during the winter months, to strong gales from the westward, and much rain. The unfavourable state of the weather prolonged my stay, and frequently prevented me from landing anything for two or three consecutive days. Having now sold and discharged everything, my first care was to send home to my friend Lawrence all the money I had, except $1300, which I retained to purchase sundry small articles to fill up the brig; I also retained sufficient funds to pay all my port charges, &c, &c, while in Cadiz. I remitted $2000 to New York, by the schooner *Imperial,* Captain Gill, and also from Gibraltar, through Horatio Sprague, Esq., $5500. My freight to Alvarado, exclusive of owners' property, amounted to $3000. Besides this, I had twenty-two cabin passengers, including men, women, and children;—for these, the price of passage was, for adults $130, and half price for children and servants.

The *Nymph's* cabin was large, she having been formerly a Mobile packet. I made an arrangement with my captain and mate, for a certain gratuity, to lodge in the steerage, and had a small house built on the quarter-deck for myself, giving the passengers the whole cabin for their accommodation. Several of my passengers were gentlemen and ladies of considerable distinction, They were generally military men, and among them were a colonel, a major, two captains, and several lieutenants, and their wives—mostly natives of Caraccas and Porto Rico, who had been many years in the armies of Spain, during the peninsular wars. Though some of them were native Spaniards, all belonged to the liberal party, and were now leaving Spain to seek shelter and employment in Caraccas, Porto Rico, and other parts of Spanish America.

About ten days before leaving Cadiz, while in the midst of apparent prosperity, I received a letter from an old friend at home, giving me the melancholy intelligence that my only little daughter was no more. She died on the 18th of October, 1823, aged about eighteen months, after an illness of six weeks.— She was a promising, interesting child, and this stroke of death was to me a most severe affliction.

One little year had but just elapsed since the decease of my beloved wife, and I began sensibly to feel that:

> *'Twas ever thus; from childhood's hour*
> *I've seen my fondest hopes decay;*
> *I never loved a plant or flower*
> *But it was first to fade away;*
> *I never nursed a dear gazelle,*
> *To soothe me with its soft black eye,*
> *But when it came to know me well,*
> *And love me—it was sure to die!*

I will not indulge farther in my own grief, but again resume; the thread of my narrative.

It was a sad sight to witness the persecutions practised against the leading men of the liberal party. They were, as I have before said, flying in every direction. Some of the most talented and conspicuous men were so obnoxious to the tyrannical government of Ferdinand VII., that in many cases they were afraid to apply to the public authorities for passports. Several of my passengers were placed in this unpleasant predicament; and I was happy to have it in my power to aid them in making their escape from Cadiz. For example,— Colonel Munoz, in a sort of disguised dress, took my arm at twilight, passed through the gates of the city, and went on board my brig, where he remained quietly unobserved for two days before I left Cadiz.

A day or two previous to our sailing, Captain Letamindi of the Spanish army applied to me for a passage for himself, wife and two children. I had then eighteen passengers engaged, and had no more room in the cabin. He was extremely anxious that I should take him with his military friends. He said himself and family would lodge anywhere I should choose to place them, and put up with any kind of fare; that his means were nearly exhausted, and that he could pay me but $100 for himself and family. His friends and former companions were all anxious that he should go, but none of them were overstocked with money. They all said Captain Letamindi was an excellent man, and that his wife was a charming, lady-like person; and if I would consent to take them, they (the passengers) would club together and purchase stores for him and his family. I told Captain Letamindi, that if he and family would consent to sleep in the after-hold of the brig, I would have a room fitted up for them there, and endeavour to make them comfortable; that they should eat at the table with the cabin passengers, and, if his friends were willing to provide him with some little necessary stores, they could do so; but if this was not perfectly convenient to him, I would provide enough for every person on board. Captain Letamindi and his wife were delighted at my offer, and forthwith came on board.

We got all our stores and passengers on board on the 5th, and the next day, December 6th, at 8 o'clock in the morning, sailed from Cadiz bound for St. Thomas, after remaining in that port fifty-three days. At noon we discharged the pilot outside the harbour. Had light airs from the N.W., and fine weather. At 5 p. m., the lighthouse bore east, five leagues distant.

As usual, a large proportion of my passengers were sea-sick during the first two or three days; after which time, however, they all recovered, and appeared happy, and strove to make themselves agreeable. The winds were light, and the weather generally good for several days.

Nothing occurred worth recording until December 13th, when at 8 o'clock in the morning, we made the three islands called the Deserters, in the neighbourhood of Madeira. These islands lie in latitude 32° 22' North, longitude 16° 25' West. Three days after, *viz.*, on December 16th, at 5 o'clock in the afternoon, passed near two small islands called the Salvages. I have in a former voyage described these rock islands, and will only remark that they lie in lat. 30° 13' North, long. 15° 42' West. The next morning at 8 o'clock we saw the Peak of Tenerife, bearing S. by W., 75 miles distant; at 10, a. m., saw the island of Palma, bearing S.W., about ten leagues distant. December the 18th, at noon, passed very near the island of Gomera; the weather being fine, I ran close in shore on the S. E. side of the island, and hove too off the little harbour of St. Sebastian.

I sent the mate and two seamen, and two of our Spanish passengers, on shore, in our own boat, to get a few casks of water, and if possible, some poultry, and a sheep or two. The mate returned in about an hour without water or anything else. The Governor sent word that he had no provisions in the town, but if we could wait until the next morning, he would send into the country for sheep, poultry, and various kinds of fruit, and that we should be supplied with all the provisions and water we required. I was inclined to take him at his word and remain off the harbour until the next morning, but most of my passengers objected; they said the island belonged to Spain, and they were afraid they should be detained if once placed in the power of an ignorant Governor. I reluctantly complied with their request, and left the island and the same little port at which Columbus first touched for water and fresh provisions, in 1492, sixteen days after leaving Palos, in the bay of Cadiz. He left Gomera on the sixth of September, after remaining there sixteen days; this island lies in lat. 28° 6' North, long. 17° 8' West. The next day we took the N. E. trade-winds, and ran down to the southward and westward, precisely on the same track taken by Columbus on his first voyage to St. Salvador, in 1492.

We now had fine weather, and constant fair winds day after day. We took our meals under an awning on the quarter-deck, and everything went on pleasantly, and all appeared happy and contented. In the evening the sound of the guitar, accompanied with sweet voices, beguiled the time, and the whole scene was peace and tranquillity: I never saw a more agreeable company of passengers on ship-board than were these ladies and gentlemen. Not a word unpleasant was uttered during the whole voyage, to mar our social intercourse and friendly enjoyment. So far as my experience and observation go, the educated classes of Spain are very social and agreeable.

For many days, running down the trade winds to the westward, we averaged about 170 miles per day, scarcely shifting a sail. During this passage I had many a long conversation with Colonel Muñoz, Captain Letamindi, and the other military gentlemen passengers, on the situation of Spain, both with respect to its then moral and political position.

These gentlemen had been for many years attached to the armies of Spain, and one of them was perfectly familiar with all the court intrigue at Madrid, having been for some years attached to the royal household. It is true they all belonged to the liberal party, and appeared to have very little feeling or charity for their opponents: still they were perfectly acquainted with the state of the nation, and I have since found that their representations and prognostications were just and true. They all averred that the leaders of the liberal constitutional party had made a great mistake in exercising so much lenity towards the priests and bigots of the royal party; and in particular their famous leader, General Riego, who at one time had the supreme power in his own hands, and who boasted that he should be able to regenerate the nation, and give them a permanent constitution and a liberal government, without shedding a single drop of blood.

This visionary belief, and too much confidence in royal honour, cost him his life, and overthrew his party. Notwithstanding he had spared the life of Ferdinand the Seventh on several occasions when he was within his power, particularly in one instance when the king and General Riego were on their way from Madrid to Cadiz, and were obliged to pass through a certain town where the people were very much incensed against him, and threatened to destroy him. Ferdinand, fearing an outbreak, and trembling for his personal security, took the general by the arm, calling him his Querido Riego, and begged him for God's sake to save him from the fury of the *populace*; but mark the contrast between the conduct of a liberal, humane general, and a bigoted, hard-hearted king.

When the tables were reversed, and he and his party came into power by the assistance of the French, he ordered General Riego to be tried by a military tribunal, who condemned him to be publicly executed at Madrid. At the execution, the fury of the bigoted *populace* knew no bounds, they cut his body into a thousand pieces, and vied with each other in desecrating his remains. Even at this time many of the best patriots and the most enlightened men belonging to Spain, were hunted and pursued like wild beasts. The grand mistake the liberal party made was, in not cutting off the heads of the royal leaders, breaking up the convents, and destroying the power of the priests. Had such a man as Napoleon or Bolivar been at the head of the constitutional party, the whole nation would, long ere this period, have been radically and thoroughly regenerated.

It is vain, in an old, corrupt country like Spain, to think of a thorough and permanent reform without much blood-letting, and of this fact all the enlightened men of the nation are now fully convinced. One of these gentlemen told me that during Riego's administration, committees were appointed to visit every part of the country, and to converse with the small farmers and peasants, and endeavour to establish schools among them, to enlighten them and their children, and diffuse elementary and useful books through the whole nation. This gentleman told me he was one of the number, and that he had visited and conversed with many of the country people, and stated to them that the object of the constitutional party was to reduce their taxes, educate their children, and in every respect to benefit their condition. He said they would listen to his representations, and for a moment appear to concur with him, but at the next breath, the force of habit and superstition would predominate, and then their answer was, that all these things appeared good and fair; still, said they, we are told that the liberal party wish to destroy our faith in our holy Catholic religion, and make infidels of us and our children; and certainly, if this is the case, it is far better for us to live here in ignorance and poverty for a few years, than to have all the wealth the world can give, and then die and go to a place of torment forever.

He said it required the patience of a saint to talk with these poor ignorant people, and with old people it was a hopeless case to expect any change for the better; but when their children were removed to the towns and cities, they had been successful in training them to think a little on the subject of popular instruction, and had not France intermeddled with their quarrels—even without a master spirit at the head of the nation— they would eventually have succeeded in bringing about a general reform. These patriotic men sighed over the unhappy state of their country, and one of the ladies wept like a child when she took her last look at Cadiz. She said she loved her country, and hoped to revisit it again when God should bless them with a liberal government, founded upon just and enlightened principles.

On Wednesday, January 7th, at 4 o'clock in the morning, we made the island of Deseada, bearing west, five leagues distant. At 6, say two hours after, we saw the island of Guadaloupe. The wind was constantly from the eastward, and the weather fine, and thus we sailed down among the West Indian Islands, passing one and making another ahead, which created renewed interest to my passengers, and kept up a very pleasant excitement during the whole day.

Jan. 8th, 1824.—In the morning we passed St. Kitts, St. Eustatia, and Saba Islands. We had fresh breezes from the N. E., and fine, clear, pleasant weather. At noon, Virgin Gorda Island bore north, ten miles distant; St. Croix in sight, bearing south-west, fifteen miles distant. At 4 o'clock in the afternoon of this day, came to anchor at St. Thomas, after a passage of thirty-two days from Cadiz, and every person on board in perfect health.

Jan. 9th.—Landed all my passengers, twenty-one in number, except one, (a native of Vera Cruz, a female servant, sent from Cadiz by her friends in that city to her family in Vera Cruz.) The greater part of my passengers left St. Thomas in a few days, for Caraccas, some few went to Porto Rico and Laguira, and with the exception of three of them, whom I afterwards met, I separated with them forever. I parted with them with regret, and should be happy to meet with them, or any of them again, if chance should ever throw us together.

At St. Thomas I discharged my young captain, he being desirous to return home. I here laid in a fresh supply of cabin and ship stores, and also purchased sundry articles to dispose of at Alvarado, such as a *puncheon* of rum, a bag or two of coffee, and some other small articles. We also had some calking done on the brig, and got both pumps repaired, &c. &c, and after lying in the port of St. Thomas eight days, made sail at 7 o'clock in the morning, on the 16th of January, bound for Alvarado, in the Gulf of Mexico. For several days after leaving St. Thomas we had moderate breezes from the N. E. and E. N. E., and generally averaged about 130 miles distance per day, during a period of three or four days. We ran down to the westward, along the south coast of the islands of Porto Rico and St. Domingo, and thence along the south side of Jamaica. In this vicinity we experienced much calm weather, and were in sight of the island for the space of five days. The passage thus far had been extremely long and tedious.

On the 25th of January, a fresh breeze sprang up from the N. E., and fine weather; we now steered more to the northward, and ran through the passage between the west end of Cuba and Cape Catoche, and then along the coast of Yucatan. The *Nymph* leaked badly, and the leak appeared to increase daily. After getting clear of the north coast of Yucatan, we experienced a norther which blew with great violence; double reefed the top-sails, and furled the main-sail and try-sail, and though the wind blew tremendously, the weather was quite clear. This gale occurred on Sunday, February 1st, in lat. 22° 7' N., on the Catoche Bank, in twenty-five fathoms of water. The next day, February 2nd, the weather moderated, when we again made sail and steered on our course with light winds from the eastward.

On Friday, February 6th, made the high land on the coast of Tobasco, and the next day, February 7th, saw Point Roca Partida. The latitude of this point is 18° 43' N., long. 94° 59' W. We had, during the day, light winds from the eastward, and fine, clear, pleasant weather.

On February 9th, in the morning, we arrived off the bar of Alvarado. The entrance to the harbour lies between two sand-banks, some thirty or forty feet high. These sand-banks render Alvarado a very blind port, and I found it very difficult to discover the gap or entrance until we approached within a short distance of the bar. At one hour after noon, we took a pilot and ran over the bar, and at 3 o'clock, came to anchor, and moored ship with two bower anchors; twenty-three days from St. Thomas, all well. I felt myself extremely fortunate in getting safe into this little port; the weather was fine, with a light breeze from the N. E., and a very smooth sea. There was only ten and a half feet of water at this time on the bar, and the *Nymph* drew about ten feet, so that we had very little water to spare.

I here employed the very respectable house of Messrs. Reilly & Suberville, to assist me to transact my business. I found in this port but a small number of vessels, and nearly all of these were Americans, *viz.*: the brig *Merced,* Captain Russel, and the schooners *Dolphin,* Captain Copeland, and *Fly,* Captain Van Dine, of New York; there were also two or three small vessels from Philadelphia and Baltimore, one U. S. schooner, commanded by Lieutenant Zantzinger, and I think, two Mexican schooners, one of them was the *Anahuac,* Captain Cochran. These schooners were placed here to guard and protect the trade at Alvarado. At St. Thomas I cleared out for New Orleans as a precautionary measure, and put into this port in distress, so that if I should meet with any difficulty in consequence of my having loaded in a Spanish place, I should have liberty to leave it, and pursue my voyage to New Orleans. We had some difficulty for a day or two at the Custom-house, on the subject of allowing me to enter and discharge my cargo.

The question grew out of the construction of a decree of the Mexican Government, passed in the city of Mexico, on the 8th of last October. That decree allowed the goods and productions of Spain to be admitted into Mexican ports until four months after the passage of the act, and then declared that all the goods and productions of Spain brought into Mexico after the expiration of the four months, should be seized and confiscated to the Mexican Government. I arrived at this port on the 9th of February, one day after the expiration of the four months, but as the law was not promulgated here until the 14th of October, it still gave me four or five days to enter and discharge, and so it was finally construed and settled, that I should have liberty to discharge and sell my cargo.

The fact is, the government wanted the duties, and the people wanted the goods. In the management of this voyage, I made one grand mistake. If in lieu of sending my funds home from Cadiz, I had laid them out in the goods and products of Spain, I should have made an immense voyage for myself and my friend. The small amount that I invested for paper, oil, raisins, &c, in Cadiz, say about $1,300, sold here for 4,200, and netted, after paying duties, commissions and all other charges, $3,500. Barrels of wine that cost $9, were here worth from $35 to $40; small barrels of brandy were worth $50 per barrel. Oil that cost in Cadiz $1 per jar, was here worth from $5 to $6; paper that cost in Cadiz $2 per ream, brought $7; raisins that cost but 90 cents per box, I sold for $3, and almost every other article in a like proportion. The whole country appeared to be quite bare of the goods and productions of Spain, and my little cargo commanded almost any price.

At this period, the castle of San Juan de Ulloa was in possession of a Spanish garrison, and no vessels were allowed to enter the harbour of Vera Cruz; consequently the whole commerce of Vera Cruz was carried on through Alvarado;—this was the nearest port, and could only be entered by small vessels. The castle of San Juan de Ulloa was at war with all Mexico, it being at this time the last and only place where the Spanish flag was flying on the continent of America, except Callao, the seaport of Lima.

I had now, after some difficulty, obtained permission to land my cargo, and early in the morning, on the 11th of February, commenced landing some light articles in our own boats. At noon, however, we were obliged to stop discharging and clear the decks, and prepare for a violent norther, which had commenced in good earnest. We sent down top-gallant-masts and yards, braced the lower and top-sail-yards to the wind, and then veered out a long scope of chain cable, and made every other preparation to ride out a violent gale from the north.

The U. S. schooner *Shark,* commanded by Captain Stevens, was lying at anchor at Point Liserdo, some eighteen or twenty miles distant from Alvarado, and as the Spanish garrison at San

Juan de Ulloa was at open war with Mexico, Captain Stevens was closely watching the trade, both at Vera Cruz and Alvarado. He was an active, vigilant officer; and was always ready and willing to protect his countrymen and their commercial interest. Not long previous to this period, Peter Harmony. Esq., of New York, had placed in the castle of San Juan de Ulloa a considerable amount of property, for safe keeping, and being anxious to avail himself of the influence of Captain Stevens, to recover and secure it from both of the belligerent parties, wrote to Captain Henry Russell, commanding the brig *Merced* of New York, to open a communication with the castle, through the influence of the commanding officer of the United States squadron in the Gulf of Mexico.

Captain Russell communicated his wishes to Captain Stevens, on the subject of proceeding with him to the castle of San Juan de Ulloa. Captain Stevens promptly complied with the request, and said he would proceed with him the next day. Captain Stevens was at this time at Alvarado, in his gig boat, with his second lieutenant, Mr. Hobbs, four stout seamen, and a cockswain, besides his own boat's crew. He took with him Captain Henry Russell and George Dekay, Esq. The last named gentleman went with them as interpreter, being perfectly familiar with the Spanish language. After having provided themselves with all necessary stores for the voyage, at 7 o'clock in the morning, on the 11th of Oct., they started from Alvarado in this little boat for the schooner *Shark,* then lying at anchor at Point Liserdo, in a direct line with the castle. When they left the port, the weather was fine, and not wind enough to ruffle the water. After taking leave of their countrymen on the beach, they started—to use their own words—"with light hearts and joyous spirits," alternately sailing and rowing, expecting in a few days to return and meet us, and talk over the incidents of the boat voyage to the seat of war.

They proceeded slowly on their course about twelve or fifteen miles, so that at noon they came in sight of the schooner *Shark,* lying at anchor: and now mark the change,—in an instant, as it were, the calm was succeeded by a violent norther, leaving them no alternative but to bear up and run before the wind, and endeavour to regain the little blind port of Alvarado, which was, fortunately for them, directly under their lee. They scudded for a time under bare poles, until the sea rose so high that they found it dangerous to run without something to force the boat faster than the sea, which began to comb and break over them. Captain Stevens calmly ordered his men to set a reefed fore-sail to accelerate the motion of the boat, and thus drive her like an arrow through the water. The sail was soon set, and the boat propelled by the fury of the wind, so that at times the water was some inches higher than the gunwale of the boat. Lieutenant Hobbs took his station on the look-out at the bows of the boat, supporting himself by the mast; Captain Stevens conning the cockswain at the helm; Captain Russel and Mr. Dekay sitting in the stern-sheets bailing out the water with their hats, and the men lying close down in the bottom of the boat.

It must have been a sublime sight to witness the silent and calm resignation of the whole party, to the will of Him who rules the ocean, and governs the whirlwind by his own good pleasure.

The most perfect order and self-possession prevailed; not a word was heard except from Captain Stevens to his lieutenant, to look out sharp for the bar at the entrance of the port, with now and then the words "steady, steady; thus, my boy, thus," to the man at the helm. At times the boat was forced through the water with such rapidity that there was great danger of running her under. The water was coming over the bows like a river; still it would not do to take in sail, and their only hope was in keeping the boat out of the way of the sea, and hitting the channel through the bar at the entrance of the little river, where the fury of the wind had lashed the sea into a white boiling foam. In the midst of this appalling scene, the plug got out of the bottom of the boat, when Captain Russell thrust his thumb into the hole, and it was some moments before anything else could be found to fill it.

The sea was so high, that at times, notwithstanding the rapidity of the boat's motion, the tops of the white billows were washed over their heads, the boat struggling to free itself from the weight of the water that had forced itself on board. For two hours this heroic little band contended with these dangers, until a kind Providence aided their own good judgement, and directed them to the entrance of the channel, when Lieutenant Hobbs conducted them through a little passage, between two immense breakers, and in a few moments after, they were within the bar and in the smooth water of the river.

The writer of this miraculous escape was watching, with others on the beach, and listening to the roaring of the surf and the howling of the tempest, and lamenting the sad fate of his worthy, but unfortunate countrymen, with expressions like these to each other—"Well, poor Stevens, Hobbs, Russell, and Dekay, are no doubt all gone; they are inevitably lost; they can never survive the fury and violence of this tempest; they have not had time to reach the *Shark,* and they are now all doubtless swallowed up in the foaming billows." Judge, then, what must have been our joy and delight a moment after, to behold the little boat inside the bar, and in a few moments after, in taking these half-drowned whole-souled Americans by the hand.

Those who have never witnessed such scenes, cannot fully understand and feel the full force of sympathy. The power of the pen and pencil cannot bring the subject home to the heart and soul, as the heart and eyes combined lay the whole scene open and naked before you.

During my stay at Alvarado, I had many conversations with Captain Stevens on the subject of his miraculous escape. He said that it was indeed a miracle, and that the finger of God was no doubt in it. He said that he was now more than ever convinced that man should be a religious being; that he had passed through many dangers at sea and on shore, had been in the battle and the storm, but had never felt himself in such imminent danger as in this instance. He was a brave, gallant man, and bore a conspicuous part on Lake Erie, under the heroic Perry, and I think was also engaged in other naval actions during our late war with England. I do not recollect to what part of the Union Lieutenant Hobbs belonged, I think, however, it was Virginia; he was a polished gentlemanly young man, about thirty or thirty-five years old, and an excellent officer, and won the esteem of all who knew him. Captain Stevens is now dead (in 1846), and whether Lieutenant Hobbs is still living, I know not.

The gale continued to increase, and at 3 o'clock in the afternoon it blew a perfect hurricane; at four, my brig took the ground, brought home the anchors, and drove on shore on a hard sand-bank, where she lay thumping during the whole night, and making much water.

The next day, February the 12th, the gale continued to blow with great fury from the north, our vessel still lying on the sand-bank, thumping with great violence; the wind blew so severely that it was difficult for the inhabitants to get about the town; the sand and dust were driven in clouds, and all kind of business was entirely suspended for the space of three days. Although the wind was so violent the weather was perfectly clear, and there was not a cloud to be seen in the heavens. On the 15th it moderated, and we discharged several boat-loads of cargo. The next day, February the 16th, hove the vessel off the sand-bank and moored ship, and went on discharging the remainder of the cargo, which all came out dry, and in a good condition, notwithstanding she had made so much water.

On the 18th I called a survey of ship-masters on the *Nymph*. The survey ordered the sheathing of the brig taken off the best way it could be, and the bottom calked temporarily, until it could be thoroughly and permanently done at some other port, there being no facilities for repairing ships or vessels at this place. Alvarado lies in lat. 18° 46' N., long 95° 38' W. of London; it is situated on the west bank of the river Alvarado, about one mile and a half above its mouth, and forty miles S. E. of Vera Cruz. The town is an insignificant place, with one church, and about 100 to 150 houses, most of which are one story high; it may perhaps contain about 800 to 1000 inhabitants.

The immediate vicinity is a barren sandy desert, though at

some distance from the town the land becomes very fertile and productive. After advancing a few miles up the river, it opens into a kind of salt water lake, which abounds with immense quantities of excellent oysters; wild game is also abundant, such as deer, hares, and other animals; wild ducks and sea-fowl are also numerous, and those persons who are fond of shooting find here abundant sporting. The climate is mild, and man can subsist with as little labour as in any part of the earth. The poorer classes live along the banks of the river in bamboo houses, which they erect in an hour or two; they plant their Indian corn on the banks of the river, where it grows almost without cultivation, and I am told produces abundantly; when ripe enough to gather, they go in canoes and bring it to their houses, and hang it up by the husks on poles erected upon stakes driven into the ground.

From the oyster banks, they can load a boat with fine oysters at low-water in a few minutes. The plantain trees supply them with bread, and they are absolutely the most independent people I ever met with. If required to labour in town or on ship-board, they appear very careless about it, and always make their own terms for their services. If any objection is made to the price of wages, they reply that there are fish enough in the river to supply them with food, and that God has provided them with all that is necessary for their sustenance; consequently they become very indolent, and live a drowsy, sleepy sort of life, with but little more activity than the oysters that nourish and sustain them.

By nature man is an indolent animal, and will only labour from necessity. It is true, that in cold bracing climates, where men are compelled to labour and provide for winter, the habit of daily employment becomes to them a pleasure; but it is only from habit that men like it. Witness the Indian tribes in the vast forests of North America, where they hunt the wild animals for a support;—after killing a buffalo or wild ox, they build a fire, around which they gorge themselves with the flesh of the animal, and then sleep for several days, and when roused by hunger they again pursue the chase for something to supply them with more food: so that it is in fact necessity alone that compels them to action.

I had now decided to go from this port with my brig to the Havana, and accordingly advertised for freight and passengers to that port. I wrote to my friend R. M. Lawrence, of New York, to get two thousand dollars insured on freight from this port to the Havana, on a valued policy. I ballasted the *Nymph* with sand, and got her ready for sea with all possible dispatch; settled my business with my consignees; received the amount of my proportion of the cargo sold, freight money, &c., &c.; and after getting about ten *ceroons* of cochineal, and eleven bales of red peppers on freight, with eleven cabin passengers, at one hundred dollars each, I was ready for sea.—Previous to leaving this port, however, I shipped on board the schooner *Fly,* Captain Henry Van Dine, five thousand dollars for account of R. M. Lawrence, of New York, and myself, joint owners of the brig. There remained with me about sixteen hundred dollars more, belonging to ourselves jointly, which amount I concluded to take with me to the Havana. Having arranged my business matters and got all my passengers on board, we sailed on the 11th of March for the Havana.

The next day, notwithstanding the weather was very fine and the sea smooth, the brig commenced leaking so that we found it necessary to pump every four hours.

March 13th.—Commenced with light winds from the E. S. E., with fine, clear, pleasant weather; the leak still increasing to 200 strokes the hour. My passengers were clerical men and merchants, *viz.*: six priests and friars, and the remainder merchants and shop-keepers. The priests and friars began to be alarmed at the brig's making so much water, and inquired of me the cause, and whether it was not best and more prudent to return to Alvarado. I had laid in sufficient stores and provisions for the voyage to Havana, and was very reluctant to return into port;—I had received all the passage money, and felt that it was a hard case for both parties; and was therefore determined to persevere on my course, as long as safety and prudence would authorize my doing so.

March 14th.— The leak had now increased to 260 strokes an hour: all my passengers were very much alarmed, and the, clerical gentlemen implored me to run for the first port, and offered me freely all the passage money they had paid, and were willing to sign a contract to that effect. The merchants and shopkeepers were more obstinate, and refused to give up any portion of the passage money; consequently, I told them I should pursue my course for the Havana, until it was the unanimous desire of all the passengers to return into port. That I would not retain all their passage money, but thought it but just and fair for me to retain the one-half of it; having expended about that amount for their provisions and stores;— and if they thought proper to agree to this arrangement, I would steer for the first port. They all soon came into the measure. The wind had been light from the N. E. for the last two days, and the current had swept us to the westward, so that on the 18th, four days after leaving port, we made the highlands about ten leagues to the northward of Vera Cruz. We now had fresh breezes from the northward, and fine weather. At noon, this day, passed near the castle of San Juan d'Ulloa, and attempted to gain the anchorage at the islands of Sacrificios, but could not fetch in. We then bore up for Alvarado.

The next day, March 16th, by turning and shifting the sand ballast, we found the principal leak was in the skarf of the keel. It proceeded through the opening of the skarf with great force and violence; and although we saw this frightful leak, we were not able to stop it. It appeared evident that the skarf must have been started when the brig was thumping on the sand-bank, during the severe weather of the 11th and 12th of February, and that the aperture had filled up with sand, which did not wash out until after we left Alvarado and got into clear ocean water.

On the 17th, at 11 o'clock in the forenoon, we took a pilot off Alvarado bar, the wind being then from the northward, with fine clear pleasant weather; we soon ran into port, and at 3 o'clock in the afternoon came to anchor, after an absence of a week. I now landed all my passengers, retaining the one-half of their passage money, and had no difficulty with them, as they were reasonable men, and were convinced that it was no fault of mine, but pure misfortune. I returned the goods on freight to the owners, or shippers, without any charges or expense to either party. I then noted a protest, and the next day Mr. S. Malsan, acting American consul and commercial agent at this port, appointed a survey of three experienced ship-masters, *viz.*, Captain Henry Russell, James Copeland, and Henry Van Dim, to repair on board the brig, and examine her situation, and report to him. Accordingly, these gentlemen ordered the brig hove out; I, with great difficulty, borrowed blocks from one vessel, and falls from another, and the next day managed to heave the brig down, so that the survey could examine the keel and bottom. They made the following report:—

We the undersigned, shipmasters of the United States, now in Alvarado, named and appointed by S. Malsan, acting commercial agent for the United States, at the port of Alvarado, to survey the brig *Nymph,* of New York, Coggeshall master, lately returned to this port in a leaky condition;

Report as follows:—That we have this day repaired on board said brig, and after a thorough and careful examination, found the skarf of the keel started, and otherwise much injured, the water forcing through in great quantities, and that it is impracticable to fasten and secure the same from the inside. We are therefore unanimously of opinion, that to make her seaworthy it will be absolutely necessary that the said brig should be hove keel out, the keel re-bolted and properly secured, the remainder of the sheathing taken off, bottom calked and re-sheathed. It is also our opinion that the expense of the before-mentioned repairs at this place, would far exceed the value of the vessel, it being doubtful, at the same time, whether it is possible to accomplish the necessary repairs to make the *Nymph* seaworthy, with the means and facilities that this place offers. We recommend Captain Coggeshall, therefore, to dismantle said brig *Nymph,* and dispose of the materials, *viz.*, spars, sails, cables, anchors, boats, hull, in short, all the tackle and apparel in detail, to the best advantage for whomsoever it may concern.

Witness our hand, in Alvarado, March 19th, 1824.

> Henry Russell, of Brig *Merced*.
> James Copeland, Schooner *Dolphin*.
> Henry Van Dim, Schooner *Fly*

We found the main keel of the *Nymph* in a very bad situation, the false almost entirely knocked off, and the main, amidships, broomed badly for ten or twelve feet, the skarf opened, and violently wrenched. All this damage, no doubt, occurred while she lay thumping on the sand-bank with a heavy cargo on board, on the 11th and 12th of February. Agreeably to the advice of the consul, and the official survey, I proceeded forthwith to dismantle the brig, and through Messrs. Bolls and Treat, auctioneers, sold the hull, and. also her materials in detail; paid off the officers and seamen according to law, and soon settled all my business at Alvarado.

About this period, Mr. Andrews, agent for the United States Bank, arrived from the city of Mexico, and related the following story:

> Messrs. Andrews and Crawford, of Philadelphia, were appointed agents for the United States Bank, to proceed to the city of Mexico, and there transact some important business for that institution. After having accomplished their mission, the Government furnished them with a military guard, to protect them on the road from the capital of Mexico to Alvarado. In company with these gentlemen, was the captain of a British man-of-war, then lying at anchor at Vera Cruz; the name of this gentleman I do not now recollect. The English captain and Mr. Andrews rode in a carriage, driven by a *postillion*, and Mr. Crawford on horseback alongside of the carriage.
>
> After getting down to Perote, the captain of the guard assured them that the danger was over, and there left them

to perform the remainder of the journey without a guard. Soon after leaving Perote, while travelling on the road, they were attacked by ten or twelve well-armed men in masks, mounted on fine horses. Their first act of violence was shooting Mr. Crawford through the body; this unfortunate gentleman fell to the ground bleeding profusely. They then ordered the captain and Mr. Andrews to leave the carriage, and lie flat on their faces on the ground, while they rifled the vehicle of all they could find; after having robbed them of their watches and all their money, the robbers were about to let them go, but at this moment the mail-carrier from Vera Cruz came in sight; he was mounted on horseback, and did not discover the robbers until very near the carriage, which several of them were overhauling; on rising a little hill he discovered his danger, but too late to make his escape; he however spurred his horse, and endeavoured to pass them; in an instant several of them went in pursuit; the fleet horses of the robbers soon overtook him, when they shot the unfortunate man, and left him dead in the road.

Mr. Andrews told me that while the captain and himself were lying on the ground, the robbers pricked their sides with the points of their swords, and threatened to dispatch them, accusing them of having concealed a portion of their money. Mr. Andrews said one of the gang (he thinks it was the captain) appeared to intercede for them, and told his men not to kill them, that they had taken all they had, and that it was useless to murder them. After the robbers were satisfied that they could find no more booty, they rode off and left them.

Mr. Andrews thinks, from the manner they rode and managed their arms and horses, that the whole gang were military men. As soon as the robbers were fairly out of sight, they lifted the poor wounded gentleman, who was bleeding and suffering from the effect of his wound, into the carriage, and returned slowly back to Perote. On the road, about a mile from where Mr. Crawford was shot, they saw the mail-carrier lying dead. Mr. Crawford lived but a few hours after they returned to Perote.

Alvarado was formerly a poor little fishing village, and was brought into notice from the circumstance of the castle of San Juan d' Ulloa being in the possession of Spain, so that no commerce or trade could be carried on with Vera Cruz except by land, from Alvarado. Consequently, as soon as the castle of San Juan d'Ulloa fell into the hands of the Mexicans, Alvarado naturally fell back into its former insignificance.

About the 27th of March, I got a copy of all my protests and surveys from the American Consul, and now only waited an opportunity to return home to the United States. As there was no vessel bound direct to the port of New York, I decided to return to Philadelphia in the pilot-boat schooner *Mexican,* with Captain Dawson. There were six cabin passengers, *viz.*: Mr. Andrews, R. Willing, Esq., a young Englishman by the name of Sagg, myself, and one or two other gentlemen whose names I do not recollect. The price of passage was $100, which we paid in advance.

After waiting some ten days for Captain Dawson to get ready for sea, we sailed from Alvarado about the middle of April. We encountered contrary winds in getting out of the Gulf of Mexico, and made a long and tedious voyage. I do not recollect any incident worth recording. The cabin passengers were intelligent, gentlemanly and agreeable men. We did not reach Philadelphia until the 18th of May, which made our passage about thirty-three days from Alvarado. I remained but two days in Philadelphia, and then came on to New York, and found my mother, sister, and all the rest of my friends well.

The underwriters paid our claim for the brig and freight in an off-hand, honourable manner, and although I had much trouble and anxiety on the voyage, still, it turned out a very profitable one; I was absent a few days over eight months, and with a small capital of about $10,000, cleared on the voyage just $8,000 for my friend Lawrence and myself. We settled everything to our mutual satisfaction.

It will be recollected that while lying in St. Thomas, on the 10th of January, 1824, I discharged Captain Coggeshall, at his own request. From that port he returned home to Milford, where he soon sickened and died, leaving a wife and one son.. On my return to New York, on being made acquainted with the early and unexpected death of my young friend and cousin, I wrote as applicable to him the following epitaph:

Here in this lonely, humble bed,
Where myrtle and wild roses grow,
A son of Neptune rests his head,
For, reader, 'tis his watch below.

Long hath he done his duty well
And weathered many a stormy blast;
But now, where gentle breezes swell,
He's safely moored in peace at last.

Tread lightly, sailors, o'er his grave,
His virtues claim a kindred tear;
And yet why mourn a brother brave,
Who rests from all his labours here?

And thus ends this troublesome though lucrative voyage in the brig *Nymph*.

www.ingramcontent.com/pod-product-compliance
Lightning Source LLC
Chambersburg PA
CBHW032056080426
42733CB00006B/298